2018 FIFA WORLD CUP RUSSIA™

THE OFFICIAL BOOK

This edition published in 2018 by Sevenoaks
an imprint of the Carlton Publishing Group
20 Mortimer Street, London, W1T 3JW

A CIP catalogue record for this book is available from the British Library

ISBN 978-1-78177-774-9

Editorial Director: Martin Corteel
Design Manager: Luke Griffin
Design: RockJaw Creative
Picture Research: Paul Langan
Production: Lisa Cook

Printed in Spain

2018 FIFA WORLD CUP RUSSIA™

THE OFFICIAL BOOK

KEIR RADNEDGE

2018 FIFA
WORLD
CUP
RUSSIA™
14 JUNE-15 JULY
FIFA WORLD CUP
RUSSIA 2018
© FIFA TM

CONTENTS

OPPOSITE: Legendary goalkeeper Lev Yashin leaps out of the Official Poster, designed by renowned Russian artist Igor Gurovich.

FIFA WORLD CUP
RUSSIA 2018

INTRODUCTION

The 2018 FIFA World Cup Russia™ will make history. For the first time the greatest event in football, the most widely followed sporting extravaganza on the planet, will take place in Eastern Europe – more specifically, in Russia.

ABOVE: There was plenty of entertainment for the audience in attendance before the main business of the Final Draw at the State Kremlin Palace in Moscow.

This most vast of the world's nations has been independent for less than two decades since the break-up of the former Soviet Union, but the fans' love of football has never been in any doubt, right back to the early, historic days of the game's development at the end of the nineteenth and start of the twentieth centuries.

Those were also the days when the first fledgling steps were taken to create FIFA, the world governing body that enshrined its right to organise a world championship. The World Cup was thus launched in South America, in Uruguay, in 1930, with no qualifying competition and 13 participants.

Now, less than a century later, all of FIFA's 211 member nations demand to be included in the global party, sharing in more than two years of international, intercontinental competition to narrow down the identity of the finalists.

Two newcomers, Iceland and Panama, will grace the 2018 finals. Russia has been preparing for these ever since the original hosting award in 2010, and the first taste of the excitement to come was delivered last year. At the FIFA Confederations Cup, world champions Germany defeated Chile 1-0 in the final.

For that tournament, four of the 12 stadiums in the 11 cities due to stage the World Cup were thrown open in Saint Petersburg, Moscow, Kazan and Sochi. Visiting fans had the opportunity not only to explore the fascinations and variations of the country but also to enjoy the excellent quality of the football which was on display.

Germany will be back in June to defend the World Cup, which they lifted for a fourth time in Brazil four years ago, after defeating Argentina in the iconic Maracaña Stadium. Another equally historic venue will take centre stage now: the Luzhniki Stadium in Moscow.

Match tickets for the finals, between 14 June and 15 July, have been massively oversubscribed. Fans from all around the world are happily prepared to make whatever financial sacrifices are necessary to attend the 64 matches being played out by the 32 teams on whom the world will focus.

The first World Cup in Europe since Germany in 2006 guarantees goals and glory in a vast country whose historical, cultural and tourist opportunities are akin to no other.

ABOVE: Traditional dancers perform around the FIFA World Cup Trophy on stage at the Final Draw in the State Kremlin Palace in Moscow on 1 December last year.

RUSSIA 2018
1000
ДНЕЙ ДО СТАРТА
ЧЕМПИОНАТ
МИРА ПО
ФУТБОЛУ FIFA
2018
В РОССИИ
2018
RUSSIA

Welcome to Russia

Russia has waited many years for the excitement of welcoming the football world to the sport's greatest showpiece. Finally, and for the first time, 2018 will see the duels of the FIFA World Cup™ taking place in Russia and Eastern Europe, thrilling fans across the planet at 12 venues in 11 cities. A uniquely different tournament awaits, in one of the first nations to take to the game.

LEFT: Officials, former and current players gathered by the countdown clock at Manezhnaya Square in Moscow on 18 September 2015 to celebrate 1,000 days before the opening game of the 2018 FIFA World Cup Russia.

FROM RUSSIA WITH LOVE

Thursday, 2 December 2010 was one of the proudest days in the modern history of Russian football: this was the date on which the country was awarded the right to host the FIFA World Cup™ for the first time in its history.

The process that led to celebrations across Russia took almost two years following the decision made on 20 December 2008 by the FIFA Executive Commmittee to open - according to a statement - "a simultaneous bidding process for two World Cup tournaments".

A year earlier, FIFA had decided to cancel the rotation system under which the finals had been assigned to Europe in 2006 (Germany played host), to Africa in 2010 (South Africa) and to South America in 2014 (Brazil). Hence 13 countries representing 11 bids were immediately ready and prepared to express an early interest in joining the race - Russia among them.

The 11 bidders were: England, Netherlands/Belgium, Russia and Spain/Portugal from Europe; separate bids from Mexico and the United States of America for the Confederation of North, Central American and Caribbean Association Football (CONCACAF); and Australia, Indonesia, Japan, Qatar and Korea Republic for the Asian Football Confederation (AFC).

At that point, no separation had been decided between the regions, so most of the candidates were expressing interest in both dates.

The first formal deadline for the bid process was 14 May 2010. On that date, in front of the world's media, protocol took priority as senior officials from the confirmed bidders all presented their candidacy books to FIFA, world football's governing body, based in Zurich. By now Indonesia and Mexico had withdrawn. So then there were nine . . .

In the subsequent months, an agreement between FIFA and the bidding competitors emerged that the 2018 tournament should be considered a "European World Cup" with the non-European nations contesting the right to play host to the finals in 2022.

FIFA sent a six-man inspection team to check out all nine bids and report back, in due course, to the Executive Committee, which had been scheduled to vote on both bids on 2 December. In preparation, the committee heard presentations from the five non-European bidders for 2022 on 1 December and from the four European candidates for 2018 on the morning of 2 December 2010.

BELOW: Vitaly Mutko, then Russia's Sports Minister, and forward Andrei Arshavin celebrate winning World Cup host rights.

ABOVE: The traditional "khorovod" Russian round dance was displayed during the opening ceremony of FIFA Confederations Cup Russia 2017, before the hosts defeated New Zealand 2-0 at the Saint Petersburg Stadium.

Each bid had a maximum of 30 minutes to state its case, with a maximum of five people involved in the presentation. The Russian delegation was the last to address the committee before the votes were cast by secret ballot. All eligible members - including members with a national interest and the FIFA President but not the FIFA Secretary General - were permitted to vote in both ballots. That meant there were 22 votes at stake.

The winning candidate needed to obtain an absolute majority after however many rounds of voting were needed. In each round, the bid receiving the fewest votes would drop out in sequence. The votes having been undertaken, two sealed envelopes with cards bearing the names of the two winners were then handed over for the formal announcements to the world at the Zurich Messe complex.

The Russian proposal detailed a maximum of 15 venues, including four from Moscow and the surrounding region. To simplify logistics in such a vast country, a "cluster" system of host cities was proposed, an idea not used since 1994. The Russian bid also stressed the opportunities to be accrued for the world game by taking the finals into eastern Europe for the first time. A new frontier was beckoning for FIFA and the World Cup.

In the 2018 ballot within the committee, two rounds of voting were necessary. In the first round, England finished fourth and was thus eliminated from contention with two votes. The Netherlands/Belgium bid secured four votes, Spain/Portugal seven and Russia nine.

Since Russia had not obtained an absolute majority, a second round of voting was necessary. This proved decisive. The Russian bid obtained an absolute majority of 13 votes ahead of Spain/Portugal on seven and Netherlands/Belgium on two. In a subsequent ballot among the committee, hosting rights to the 2022 World Cup were awarded to Qatar.

Vladimir Putin, then the Prime Minister of Russia, flew in to Zurich for a victorious press conference as soon as the result was declared. He promised his nation's full commitment to providing the essential infrastructure - venues, accommodation, transport facilities, etc. In addition, he promised that ticket-holding fans from abroad would be able to take advantage of a visa-free entry system and free ground transport within the Russian Federation for matches.

He said: "There are a lot of misconceptions of Russia from previous times, from the Cold War era. But come to see how we will prepare for the World Cup and you will gain a very different perception.

"You can take my word for it that the 2018 World Cup in Russia will be up to the highest standards, with new modern stadiums and facilities which will be built not only in time but to perfection."

THE VENUES

When it came to selecting a venue map for the 2018 FIFA World Cup Russia™, the Local Organising Committee faced a challenge: the vastness of the host country.

Hence Russia has adopted a variation of the cluster system employed by earlier host nations up to 1994. This regulates both travel distances and timings, which is an advantage not only for the teams but also for visiting fans who want to follow their favourites through the group stage.

The bidding proposal to FIFA was based on the concept of staging the tournament in the European segment of the Russian Federation.

Initial proposals featured the potential use of up to 16 stadiums, including four in the capital, Moscow, and surrounding region. Subsequent consideration led to the allocation of matches to two Moscow venues and the withdrawal of proposals to include the cities of Yaroslavl, north-east of Moscow, and Krasnodar in the south.

Ekaterinburg is the furthest eastern point of the World Cup map while the Baltic exclave of Kaliningrad is the western extreme. Kaliningrad thus makes up the Northern Cluster in tandem with Saint Petersburg, whose new stadium played a central role in the FIFA Confederations Cup Russia 2017.

At the opposite end of the country, the Southern Cluster comprises the new venue in Rostov-on-Don plus the Fisht Stadium in subtropical Sochi on the Black Sea. The Fisht Stadium played a dramatic role as the venue for the opening and closing ceremonies in the city's hosting of the Winter Olympics in early 2014. It also hosted four matches in the Confederations Cup, including a semi-final in which Germany defeated Mexico 4-1.

The busiest grouping of stadiums is the Volga Cluster, which features five venues stretching down from Nizhny Novgorod to Saransk and Kazan, then Samara and Volgograd itself. Kazan, considered the "Sports Capital" of the Russian Federation, played an important role in the Confederations Cup. The Kazan Arena hosted four matches, including the second semi-final, in which Portugal defeated Chile in a penalty shoot-out.

Ultimately all World Cup roads lead back to Moscow, where the finals open on 14 June. Moscow is the only city to provide two stadiums in what is termed the Central Cluster. One is the new home of FC Spartak Moscow, and staged four matches in the Confederations Cup. The other is the historic and world-famous Luzhniki Stadium.

Luzhniki will be the focus of the entire football world as the venue for the opening match and the final as well as five other matches. It was built in the mid-1950s with an original capacity of more than 100,000. Major redevelopment means a new capacity of 81,006 for the stadium, which has, down the years, hosted the majority of home matches of the Russian national team. It was also the venue for the finals of the 2008 UEFA Champions League and the 1999 UEFA Cup [now the UEFA Europa League].

Bidding documents promised stadiums containing the latest technological developments, and purpose-built to meet all of FIFA's space requirements, as well as offering the highest safety and hospitality standards and answering the legacy needs of the host cities for use after the tournament.

The new generation of venues are contributing to the Russian Federation's plan to step up investment in sports infrastructure. This is expected to encourage even greater participation in sport in general as well as a steady increase in attendances at premier and first league matches - and, in the words of the Local Organising Committee, to offer "an extraordinary experience for the players and fans".

OPPOSITE: The Telstar 18 is the Official Match Ball for the 2018 FIFA World Cup Russia. Alongside it at the Luzhniki Stadium in Moscow is the FIFA World Cup trophy.

adidas
RUSSIA 2018
TELSTAR
18
OFFICIAL
MATCH BALL
FIFA
WORLD CUP

KALININGRAD

The Kaliningrad Stadium will host four matches in the group stage. The five-storey, multisport stadium in the Baltic exclave has been built on the shores of Oktyabrsky Island, near the Pregola river. After the World Cup, capacity will be trimmed to 25,000 while a surrounding residential development will feature parks, quays and embankments. The stadium is a half-hour walk from Kant Island, named in honour of the philosopher Immanuel Kant, who is buried in a mausoleum standing beside the fourteenth-century cathedral. Kaliningrad, formerly Königsberg, is separated from the rest of the Russian land mass by parts of Lithuania and Belarus. It has a common frontier with Poland in the south.

Host city: Kaliningrad (population 467,000)
Stadium capacity: 35,212 (new)
Home team: FC Baltika Kaliningrad

MOSCOW (LUZHNIKI)

The Luzhniki Stadium in the Russian capital of Moscow is one of the world's most historic sports arenas. It was built originally in 450 days to host the first nationwide summer *Spartakiad* in 1956. Since then, the Luzhniki complex has hosted a multitude of major sporting and cultural events, including the 1980 Summer Olympics and various world championships in other sports as well as more than 3,000 football matches. The Luzhniki has staged most of the home matches played by the Russian national football team, and has served, at various times, as home to three of the city's football clubs: Spartak Moscow, PFC CSKA Moscow and Torpedo Moscow. It has also hosted the finals of the UEFA Champions League in 2008 and the UEFA Cup in 1999. Redevelopment of the Luzhniki, after Russia won the hosting rights to the FIFA World Cup, began in 2013. This involved preserving the historical façade of the stadium, which is one of Moscow's landmarks. The athletics track has been removed, while the stands have been shifted closer to the pitch and converted to a rectangular shaping which features the addition of two extra tiers.

Host city: Moscow (population 12.2m)
Stadium capacity: 81,006 (redeveloped)
Home team: Russian national team

ROSTOV-ON-DON

The Rostov Arena is the new pride of the administrative capital of the Southern Federal District and the Rostov Region. The Rostov-on-Don stadium has been sited on the left bank of the river and is an additional key feature close to a long waterfront with countless restaurants, cafés, clubs and hotels - amenities which traditionally attract both local residents and visitors. The design of the stadium was devised specifically to imitate the meanderings of the river. The varying heights of the stands allow spectators a first-class view of the action on the pitch as well as views of Rostov-on-Don itself.

Host city: Rostov-on-Don (population 1.1m)
Stadium capacity: 45,145 (new)
Home team: FC Rostov

EKATERINBURG

The Ekaterinburg Arena is home to one of Russia's oldest football clubs, FC Ural, and was built originally in 1953. Since then, it has been redeveloped several times, most recently in 2011. Each time great care was taken to maintain the stadium's historic façade. A decorative design typical of Soviet neo-Classicism was applied in the construction of the stands, along with decorative art in the form of sculptures, vases and banners. The upgraded stadium retains the historical façade with a roof and temporary stands being installed especially for the tournament.

Host city: Ekaterinburg (population 1.4m)
Stadium capacity: 35,696
Home team: FC Ural

NIZHNY NOVGOROD

The new stadium in Nizhny Novgorod, formerly Gorky, has been built in one of the city's most picturesque locations, at the confluence of the Volga and Oka rivers, near the Alexander Nevsky Cathedral. The stadium design was inspired by the two key natural aspects of the Volga region - water and wind - but is careful not to compromise the historic districts surrounding it. The stadium will host six matches in the finals, including one in the round of 16 and one quarter-final.

Host city: Nizhny Novgorod (population 1.2m)
Stadium capacity: 45,331 (new)
Home team: FC Olympiets Nizhny Novgorod

KAZAN

The Kazan Arena is only five years old but has already attained international sports renown. It was built for the 2013 Summer Universiade and also hosted the opening and closing ceremonies. Two years later, Kazan Arena was the prime venue of the FINA World Aquatics Championships. Hence the venue, inspired by a water lily, is the world's only football stadium also to have witnessed 12 world swimming records. The first football match was staged in August 2013, when FC Rubin Kazan drew 1-1 with FC Lokomotiv Moscow. As well as football and other sports events, the stadium hosts concerts and cultural events. Local training sites in the capital of the Tatar Republic include the central Electron Stadium, the training base of FC Rubin Kazan, and the Central Stadium, which was the club's home when they won the Russian championship in 2008 and 2009.

Host city: Kazan (population 1.2m)
Stadium capacity: 44,779
Home team: FC Rubin Kazan

SAMARA

The Samara Arena is a significant addition to the modernistic features of a city which, as well as being the region's administrative capital, is a major economic centre, transportation hub and cultural magnet for the Volga basin. Samara, formerly Kuybyshev, emerged in the 1950s as the leading centre of Soviet airspace and rocket engineering. The world's first satellite and the world's first manned spaceship, piloted by Yuri Gagarin, were launched from craft designed and built in Kuybyshev. Hence the design concept for the new arena is dominated by the theme of space, and the Samara Arena resembles a glass dome. On 21 July 2014, Russian President Vladimir Putin took part in a time-capsule ceremony marking the start of construction. After the finals, the stadium will be home to FC Krylia Sovetov. Training venues include the club's old Metallurg Stadium home.

Host city: Samara (population 1.1m)
Stadium capacity: 44,807
Home team: FC Krylia Sovetov

SARANSK

Saransk's Mordovia Arena stands in the Oktyabrsky district on the banks of the Insar and is named in honour of the surrounding region. Work began in 2010, the 1,000th anniversary of the unification of the Mordovian people with Russia's other ethnic groups. The stadium has been designed in the shape of an oval featuring a bright range of colours, including orange, red and white to match the distinctive palette of Mordovia's arts and crafts. Temporary structures built for the finals will be removed after completion of the match schedule, reducing stadium capacity to 25,000. The vacated space will be used for indoor volleyball, basketball and tennis courts, as well as fitness centres. Training venues include the Olympic Centre, Start Stadium and FC Mordovia Stadium. After the finals, the stadium will become the new home of FC Mordovia Saransk.

Host city: Saransk (population 315,000)
Stadium capacity: 44,442 (new)
Home team: FC Mordovia Saransk

SOCHI

The Fisht Stadium in Sochi is one of the remarkable sports venues developed after the elongated city on the Black Sea won hosting rights to the 2014 Winter Olympics. Supporting infrastructure included hundreds of kilometres of roads, along with transport hubs, airports, concert venues, museums and dozens of hotels. The Fisht Stadium hosted both the opening and closing ceremonies of the Games and was thus introduced via television coverage to more than 30 million sports fans around the world. Subtropical Sochi hosted its first Formula 1 race that same year, and has since hosted more than 300 major sports events. The Fisht Stadium, in the Olympic Park in Imeretin Valley, was named after a peak in the western part of the Greater Caucasus Mountain Range. "Fisht" means "white head" in the Adyghe language. Temporary stands have been added at each end of the stadium for the FIFA World Cup. Training venues include Adler-1 and Adler-2 as well as the Park Arena in the Olympic Park.

Host city: Sochi (population 412,000)
Stadium capacity: 47,700
Home team: Russian national team

VOLGOGRAD

The Volgograd Arena has been built on the site of the former historic Central Stadium, at the foot of the Mamayev Kurgan war memorial. That old stadium was built in 1962, on the site of a former oil depot. The new stadium's façade is shaped like an inverted, lattice-work cone, and its design was inspired by aspects of a Victory Day firework display. During the finals, the Volgograd Arena will play host to four group matches. After the competition, the stadium, which stands on the banks of Europe's longest river, will be a new home to FC Rotor Volgograd.

Host city: Volgograd (population 1.1m)
Stadium capacity: 45,568 (new)
Home team: FC Rotor Volgograd

MOSCOW (SPARTAK)

Spartak Stadium was completed in 2014, a historic day for FC Spartak Moscow. Previously Spartak had never had a stadium to call their own. Spartak, founded in 1922, had played their home matches at a variety of major arenas including the Luzhniki, Dynamo, Lokomotiv and the Eduard Streltsov Stadium. In 2006, the club secured the necessary land on the site of Moscow's old airfield in the district of Tushino. Ground was broken a year later, on 2 June 2007. Construction began in 2010 and the official first match saw Spartak draw 1-1 with Red Star Belgrade on 5 September 2014. A week earlier two Spartak veterans' teams had contested a trial match. The most notable feature for fans approaching the stadium is the giant, 24-metre gladiator statue of Spartacus towering over the main entrance. A pitchside monument celebrates the founders of Spartak, the four Starostin brothers: Nikolai, Andrey, Aleksandr and Pyotr. A monument in honour of former Spartak midfielder Fyodor Cherenkov was unveiled near the stadium in 2015. A residential development is planned for construction after the finals. Training venues include the Arena CSKA, Spartak's primary training facility, and the nearby stadium at Ulitsa Vasiliya Botyleva.

Host city: Moscow (population 12.2m)
Stadium capacity: 43,298 (new)
Home team: FC Spartak Moscow

SAINT PETERSBURG

The Saint Petersburg Stadium, on Krestovsky Island to the west of the city, will stage seven matches in the World Cup finals, including one semi-final and the third-place play-off. The cultural capital of Russia is already familiar to football fans around the world after hosting four matches at last year's FIFA Confederations Cup. These included the opening match and the final. Saint Petersburg, located on the Gulf of Finland coast and at the mouth of the Neva, is one of the world's great tourist attractions with its multiplicity of bridges crossing 64 rivers, 48 canals and 34 streams with a total length of 160 kilometres. The new venue has replaced the historic SM Kirov Stadium, and has been hailed as one of the most technologically sophisticated sports arenas in Europe. Its retractable roof takes only 15 minutes to open or close. The arena, which can also host concerts and other entertainment, will be the new home of FC Zenit. Training venues include Zenit Academy's Smena Stadium as well as the club's old Petrovsky Stadium home and the Turbostroitel Stadium.

Host city: Saint Petersburg (population 5.2m)
Stadium capacity: 68,134 (new)
Home team: FC Zenit Saint Petersburg

RUSSIA'S FOOTBALL HERITAGE

Russia's football story is a long and impressive one, stretching back to 1887 when the game was introduced by Britons Clement and Harry Charnock. Their family managed the Morozov cotton mills in Orekhovo Zuyevo, some 50 miles to the east of Moscow.

The Charnocks organised teams and provided the footballs and blue-and-white shirts in the colours of their favourite club back home, Blackburn Rovers. At the same time, students were coming home to Saint Petersburg from Britain with this new craze. Clubs were launched there in schools and in military academies, the oldest being the Saint Petersburg Circle of Amateur Sportsmen, founded in 1897.

A league was launched in Saint Petersburg before the end of the nineteenth century and a Moscow league in 1901. Attendances at some matches of between 10,000 and 15,000 were recorded. An initial Russian Football Association was founded in 1912 and joined FIFA in time to send a national team to the Olympic Games that year in Stockholm. Russia were defeated 2-1 by Finland in the quarter-finals and then 16-0 by Germany in an unofficial consolation tournament. It was a start.

The succeeding few years saw regional leagues springing up throughout the country in the major cities of what would become, after all the revolutionary upheavals, the Soviet Union.

In the international political turmoil of the 1920s, Russian or Soviet sports teams remained absent from the expanding international arena. Domestically, the same decade saw the creation of clubs such as Dynamo Moscow, Spartak, Torpedo and CSKA, which would become pillars of the communist recreational structures.

ABOVE: England captain Billy Wright and the Soviet Union's Nikita Simonyan pose for the cameras before the 1958 FIFA World Cup duel.

The restructuring of domestic sport led, in due course, to the creation of a national league and cup competition in 1936. The league was split into spring and autumn competitions, which were won, respectively, by Dynamo Moscow and Spartak Moscow. The cup was won by the railway workers' club, Lokomotiv Moscow.

An outstanding player was Dynamo's goalscoring forward Mikhail Yakushin. He was later the manager of the Dynamo team that caused a sensation with their performances and results during a legendary tour of Britain and Sweden in the winter of 1945.

An unofficial national team had played a handful of matches in the 1920s, and an official Soviet team was created for the football tournament for the 1952 Summer Olympics in Helsinki. The team, including future World Cup stars in half-back Igor Netto and winger

Anatoli Ilyin, defeated Bulgaria 2-1 in a preliminary round, then lost a first-round replay to Yugoslavia. The first meeting ended in a 5-5 draw after extra time, the captain, Bobrov, scoring a hat-trick to bring the team back from 5-1 down. Yugoslavia won the replay 3-1.

Four years later, in 1956, a Soviet team of legends - not only Netto but also goalkeeper Lev Yashin and centre-forward Nikita Simonyan - won the Olympic gold medal in Melbourne. In the final at the Melbourne Cricket Ground, they defeated Yugoslavia by 1-0 with a goal from Ilyin.

This served as a stepping stone towards a World Cup debut for the Soviet Union in 1958. Yashin and his team-mates reached the quarter-finals in Sweden before their adventure ended with a 2-0 defeat by their hosts. Two years later, they maintained their progress at elite level by winning the inaugural UEFA European Championship, then known as the Nations Cup. Again they defeated Yugoslavia in the final, winning 2-1 after extra time. Slava Metreveli and Viktor Ponedelnik scored the goals in the old Parc des Princes in Paris.

The Soviet Union were now acknowledged as a major force at national team level. They lost to hosts Chile in the quarter-finals of the 1962 World Cup and then finished a best-ever fourth in the finals in England in 1966. In this era they were also European Championship runners-up three times - in 1964 in Spain, in 1972 in Belgium and in 1988 in West Germany - as well as fourth in 1968 in Italy.

In the 1970s and 1980s, the Soviet style of football evolved from the physical Russian game by embracing the more technical styles developed among the key players of Ukraine's Dynamo Kiev and Georgia's Dinamo Tbilisi.

In 1975, Kiev's Oleg Blokhin was voted European Footballer of the Year, as had been Yashin in 1963 and as would be Kiev's Igor Belanov in 1986. Blokhin remains the leading marksman in Soviet history with 42 goals in 112 internationals. He was the only player to achieve a century of caps for the Soviet Union.

After the end of the communist era, the Soviet Union morphed into the Commonwealth of Independent States at the 1992 European Championship finals. Subsequently the newly independent Russian Federation assumed the Soviet Union's place in the international game.

The Russian national team has not always managed to reach the finals of the FIFA World Cup and has been seen more often in the latter stages of the UEFA European Championship.

Teams managed by Pavel Sadyrin, Oleg Romantsev and the Italian Fabio Capello were eliminated in the group stage of the World Cups in 1994, 2002 and 2014. Between 1996 and 2016, Russia qualified five times for the finals of the European Championship.

The one occasion in which Russia have progressed beyond a group stage was the 2008 European Championship when the team, under the management of Guus Hiddink, reached the semi-finals.

BELOW LEFT: Lev Yashin saves from Portugal's Eusebio in the third-place play-off at the 1966 FIFA World Cup at Wembley.

BELOW: Oleg Blokhin played for the Soviet Union at the 1982 and 1986 FIFA World Cup finals and was coach of Ukraine at 2006 FIFA World Cup Germany.

The Road to Russia

Russian fans have waited many years to welcome the FIFA World Cup™ to the largest country on the planet, more than twice the size of 2014 host Brazil. The finals are being staged in the European western segment of the Russian Federation. This still means a wide, exciting spread of the drama from Saint Petersburg in the north to Sochi in the south, from Kaliningrad in the west to Ekaterinburg in the east.

LEFT: The Kremlin in Moscow will provide one of the most dramatic of scenic backdrops for the FIFA World Cup once the tournament opens on 14 June.

THE QUALIFIERS: EUROPE

Nine European teams which competed at the last FIFA World Cup™ in Brazil are back to play at the 2018 finals. This follows a 14-month qualifying campaign, which began on 4 September 2016 and concluded on 14 November 2017.

The greatest surprises were reserved until the last weeks, which confirmed the absence from the finals of four-time world champions Italy and three-time runners-up the Netherlands.

A record 54 nations entered the European adventure. Only Russia, as hosts, were already assured of their presence in the finals. Gibraltar and Kosovo made their FIFA World Cup debuts in the qualifying competition after only four months as members of FIFA, having been admitted by the Congress in Mexico City in May 2016.

The European campaign began less than two months after the conclusion of the UEFA European Championship, in which Portugal had defeated hosts France. Only the winners of the nine groups of six teams were assured of a place in the finals; the remaining four European slots were decided by two-leg play-offs between the eight best second-placed teams. These were chosen after excluding results against the last team in each group.

A "group of death" status was awarded to Group G, which included two former world champions in Spain (2010) and Italy (1934, 1938, 1982 and 2006).

Reigning world champions Germany were the only team to complete their programme with a 100% record, winning all ten matches. Coach Joachim Löw's team scored 43 goals and conceded only four. Remarkably, Germany's goals were shared among 22 players (including one own goal). Their top marksmen, Thomas Müller and Sandro Wagner, scored a modest five goals apiece. The Germans were joint-leading scorers with Belgium, for whom Romelu Lukaku bagged 11 goals in Group H.

Even more miserly defensive records than Germany's four goals were the minimal three conceded by England in Group F and Spain in Group G.

The leading individual marksman was Robert Lewandowski, the Polish captain, who led his team's qualifying effort by example with 16 goals. Cristiano Ronaldo, heading along the path to further best player awards from FIFA for both 2016 and 2017, was hot in pursuit with 15 goals.

The two players thus renewed a particular rivalry. Lewandowski set a record for the FIFA World Cup's European qualifying competition as both he and Ronaldo overhauled the 14-goal mark set by Yugoslavia's

BELOW: Jonny Evans (left) and Thomas Müller tussle for possession during Germany's 3-1 qualifying group victory over Northern Ireland in Belfast last October.

ABOVE: Iceland's players and coaching staff celebrate with fans in the centre of Reykjavik after becoming the smallest country ever – in terms of population – to qualify for the finals of the FIFA World Cup.

Predrag Mijatović in the 1998 preliminaries. Even so, Ronaldo attained a record of his own: he has scored more goals (30) than any other European player in FIFA World Cup qualifying history.

The European group winners featured four past world champions – Germany, France, England and Spain – as well as three former semi-finalists – Portugal, also the 2016 European champions, as well as Poland and Belgium. The other two nations heading directly for Russia were Serbia and Iceland. The latter lit up the UEFA European Championship by reaching the quarter-finals for the first time, and in Russia their adventure will continue.

Notable absentees after the group stage were the Netherlands, who had been third in Brazil in 2014. The *Oranje* were eliminated after goal difference saw them edged into third place in Group A by Sweden.

Slovakia were the second-placed team (behind England in Group F) who failed to make the cut into the play-offs, where Switzerland, Italy, Denmark, Croatia, Sweden, Northern Ireland, Greece and the Republic of Ireland were seeded according to their places in the FIFA/Coca-Cola World Ranking.

The first legs saw both Croatia and Switzerland take significant command of their destiny. Croatia defeated Greece 4-1 at home with goals from Luka Modric´, Nikola Kalinic´, Ivan Perišic´ and Andrej Kramaric´, while the Swiss ground out a 1-0 victory away to Northern Ireland courtesy of a Ricardo Rodríguez penalty, which the Irish players disputed in vain.

The other two ties remained wide open after Sweden edged Italy 1-0 with a goal from substitute Jakob Johansson in Stockholm while Denmark drew 0-0 with the Republic of Ireland in front of their own fans in Copenhagen.

In the return ties, Switzerland made up for earlier disappointment. A last-game defeat by Portugal saw them miss out on direct qualification, but by holding Northern Ireland goalless they now won 1-0 on aggregate. Greece and Croatia were also goalless in Piraeus, which presented the visitors with progress 4-1 overall.

In Dublin, the Republic of Ireland took a step towards the finals when Shane Duffy put them ahead against Denmark, but the visitors recovered superbly to win and progress 5-1 courtesy of a hat-trick by Christian Eriksen.

On the previous evening, Italian football had been left reeling after the failure of the *Azzurri* to score at home in the Stadio Giuseppe Meazza in Milan. Veteran goalkeeper-captain Gigi Buffon charged upfield twice at corners in stoppage time, but in vain as Janne Andersson's men reached the finals 1-0 on aggregate. Italy were left to rue only their second-ever absence from the finals and their first qualifying exit since 1958.

THE QUALIFIERS: REST OF THE WORLD

Two newcomers will play at the 2018 FIFA World Cup Russia™: Iceland and Panama. A dramatic CONCACAF qualifying tournament saw the United States fail to qualify for the first time since 1986, and Panama emerged for the first time.

The North and Central America and Caribbean region process involved all 35 of its FIFA-affiliated nations playing three knockout rounds, with the top-ranked nations joining for the subsequent two group-stage rounds. Knockout competition opened on 22 March 2015, and the fourth-round three-group section on 13 November.

Mexico, Honduras, Costa Rica, the United States, Panama and Trinidad & Tobago took the top slots in the three groups to set up the concluding six-team set. Canada fell by the wayside after finishing third behind Mexico and Honduras in Group A.

The headline duel matched old rivals USA and Mexico, who met immediately. *El Tri* posted a 2-1 victory away in Columbus, Ohio, and worse was to follow for the USA: a 4-0 defeat in Costa Rica prompted the replacement of coach Jürgen Klinsmann with FIFA World Cup old hand Bruce Arena.

They could have recovered. By the last round of matches, Mexico and Costa Rica were already through to Russia with the third finals slot open to any two out of Panama, Honduras and the USA. Panama and Honduras won their last matches against Costa Rica and Mexico respectively, and the USA could have overtaken both by winning away to Trinidad & Tobago. Instead, they lost 2-1 to the bottom team to finish fifth and miss out.

Honduras also fell short after losing their intercontinental play-off 3-1 on aggregate against Australia from the Asian Football Confederation.

The AFC had doubled the FIFA World Cup qualifying tournament with preliminaries for the Asian Cup. The first two rounds were played on

BELOW: Forward Mohamed Salah is hailed by the fans in Alexandria after his penalty in a 2-1 defeat of Congo lifted Egypt into the finals for the first time since 1990.

ABOVE: Omar Al Soma of Syria (right) celebrates with Tamer Mohamed after his goal had given Syria an early lead in their Asian play-off second leg against Australia in Sydney; unfortunately for the Syrians they went on to lose after extra time.

a direct elimination basis and Quito (Chiquito do Carmo) of Timor-Leste wrote his name into history, scoring the first goal in the entire tournament in a 4-1 defeat of Mongolia in Dili on 12 March 2015.

A two-group third round saw the two top teams from each section (IR Iran and Korea Republic plus Japan and Saudi Arabia) reach the finals while third-placed Syria and Australia duelled over the right to enter the intercontinental play-offs.

Syria's campaign was remarkable, considering the warfare ravaging the region. They finished as runners-up to Japan in their second-round group thanks to the seven-goal leadership of Saudi-based forward Omar Maher Kharbin, whose achievements earned him the 2017 Asian Footballer of the Year award.

Syria went so close in the play-off. They drew 1-1 in their "alternative" home leg in Malaysia, then lost 2-1 (and 3-2 on aggregate) in Sydney only after extra time. The *Socceroos* went on to defeat Honduras and claim a fifth AFC slot in the finals.

The other intercontinental play-off matched New Zealand, undefeated winners in Oceania, against Peru, who had finished fifth in the South American section. The Peruvians claimed a goalless draw in Wellington, then won 2-0 back in Lima. Goals from Jefferson Farfán and Christian Ramos lifted them into the finals for the first time in 36 years.

South America's pathway saw all ten members of the Confederación Sudamericana de Fútbol CONMEBOL play each other home and away in a *liguilla* (little league) from which the top four progressed directly to the finals in Russia. The fifth-placed team - Peru, as it turned out - entered the intercontinental play-offs.

Brazil, five-time record world champions and also newly crowned Olympic gold medallists, won the group with ease with four matches to spare. New coach Tite instilled a new aura of confidence after disappointing results in the *Copa América* and initial FIFA World Cup qualifiers under former Cup-winning captain Dunga.

The Brazilians had opened with a 2-0 defeat away to South American champions Chile but, by the end of the campaign, their fortunes had reversed. Chile failed to qualify while Brazil were ten points clear of runners-up Uruguay after scoring 41 goals and conceding 11. Gabriel Jesus was their seven-goal top scorer, supported by Neymar and Paulinho with five apiece.

With Uruguay virtually certain of qualifying, the other two automatic slots and play-off places were wide open ahead of the last round. Argentina, after a poor start, improved to finish third, while Colombia finished fourth after a 1-1 draw away to fifth-placed Peru. Chile, South American champions and runners-up three months earlier in the FIFA Confederations Cup, missed out altogether on a return to Russia.

Africa will have five nations at the finals after a two-year qualification phase. The 54 teams of the Confederation of African Football played out a three-round tournament: two knockout sections and then a final stage with five groups of four teams each. The knockout rounds proved the end of the line for 2006 finalists Togo, who lost 4-0 on aggregate to Uganda.

In the decisive group stage, Tunisia topped Group A by only one point from Congo DR, but Nigeria, Morocco, Senegal and Egypt were all decisive winners. Former finalists such as Cameroon, Algeria, Côte d'Ivoire, South Africa and Ghana all fell short. Egypt's Mohamed Salah and Préjuce Nakoulma of Burkina Faso were the leading marksmen in the group stage, scoring five goals each.

QUALIFYING RESULTS AND TABLES

AFRICA
Round 3

Group A

	MP	W	D	L	GF	GA	+/-	Pts
Tunisia	6	4	2	0	11	4	7	14
Congo DR	6	4	1	1	14	7	7	13
Libya	6	1	1	4	4	10	-6	4
Guinea	6	1	0	5	6	14	-8	3

Group B

	MP	W	D	L	GF	GA	+/-	Pts
Nigeria	6	4	1	1	11	6	5	13
Zambia	6	2	2	2	8	7	1	8
Cameroon	6	1	4	1	7	9	-2	7
Algeria	6	1	1	4	6	10	-4	4

Nigeria's 1-1 draw with Algeria was awarded 3-0 to Algeria because of an ineligible player.

Group C

	MP	W	D	L	GF	GA	+/-	Pts
Morocco	6	3	3	0	11	0	11	12
Côte d'Ivoire	6	2	2	2	7	5	2	8
Gabon	6	1	3	2	2	7	-5	6
Mali	6	0	4	2	1	9	-8	4

Group D

	MP	W	D	L	GF	GA	+/-	Pts
Senegal	6	4	2	0	10	3	7	14
Burkina Faso	6	2	3	1	10	6	4	9
Cape Verde	6	2	0	4	4	12	-8	6
South Africa	6	1	1	4	7	10	-3	4

Group E

	MP	W	D	L	GF	GA	+/-	Pts
Egypt	6	4	1	1	8	4	4	13
Uganda	6	2	3	1	3	2	1	9
Ghana	6	1	4	1	7	5	2	7
Congo	6	0	2	4	5	12	-7	2

QUALIFIED: Tunisia, Nigeria, Morocco, Senegal, Egypt

SOUTH AMERICA
Round 1

	MP	W	D	L	GF	GA	+/-	Pts
Brazil	18	12	5	1	41	11	30	41
Uruguay	18	9	4	5	32	20	12	31
Argentina	18	7	7	4	19	16	3	28
Colombia	18	7	6	5	21	19	2	27
Peru	18	7	5	6	27	26	1	26
Chile	18	8	2	8	26	27	-1	26
Paraguay	18	7	3	8	19	25	-6	24
Ecuador	18	6	2	10	26	29	-3	20
Bolivia	18	4	2	12	16	38	-22	14
Venezuela	18	2	6	10	19	35	-16	12

South America/Oceania Intercontinental Play-Off

New Zealand 0-0 **Peru**
Peru 2-0 New Zealand
Peru won 2-0 on aggregate

QUALIFIED: Brazil, Uruguay, Argentina, Colombia, Peru

RIGHT: Left to right, Peru's Raul Ruidiaz, Jefferson Farfan and Christian Cueva savour World Cup qualification after defeating New Zealand 2-0.

ASIA
Round 3

Group A

	MP	W	D	L	GF	GA	+/-	Pts
IR Iran	10	6	4	0	10	2	8	22
Korea Republic	10	4	3	3	11	10	1	15
Syria	10	3	4	3	9	8	1	13
Uzbekistan	10	4	1	5	6	7	-1	13
China PR	10	3	3	4	8	10	-2	12
Qatar	10	2	1	7	8	15	-7	7

Group B

	MP	W	D	L	GF	GA	+/-	Pts
Japan	10	6	2	2	17	7	10	20
Saudi Arabia	10	6	1	3	17	10	7	19
Australia	10	5	4	1	16	11	5	19
United Arab Emirates	10	4	1	5	10	13	-3	13
Iraq	10	3	2	5	11	12	-1	11
Thailand	10	0	2	8	6	24	-18	2

Asian Play-Off

Syria 1-1 **Australia**
Australia 2-1 Syria (after extra time)
Australia won 3-2 on aggregate

CONCACAF/Asia Intercontinental Play-Off

Honduras 0-0 **Australia**
Australia 3-1 Honduras
Australia won 3-1 on aggregate

QUALIFIED: IR Iran, Korea Republic, Japan, Saudi Arabia, Australia

BELOW: Australia captain Mile Jedinak (15) celebrates one of his three goals which beat Honduras 3-1 in Sydney in the second leg of their intercontinental play-off.

EUROPE

Group A

	MP	W	D	L	GF	GA	+/-	Pts
France	10	7	2	1	18	6	12	23
Sweden	10	6	1	3	26	9	17	19
Netherlands	10	6	1	3	21	12	9	19
Bulgaria	10	4	1	5	14	19	-5	13
Luxembourg	10	1	3	6	8	26	-18	6
Belarus	10	1	2	7	6	21	-15	5

Group B

	MP	W	D	L	GF	GA	+/-	Pts
Portugal	10	9	0	1	32	4	28	27
Switzerland	10	9	0	1	23	7	16	27
Hungary	10	4	1	5	14	14	0	13
Faroe Islands	10	2	3	5	4	16	-12	9
Latvia	10	2	1	7	7	18	-11	7
Andorra	10	1	1	8	2	23	-21	4

Group C

	MP	W	D	L	GF	GA	+/-	Pts
Germany	10	10	0	0	43	4	39	30
Northern Ireland	10	6	1	3	17	6	11	19
Czech Republic	10	4	3	3	17	10	7	15
Norway	10	4	1	5	17	16	1	13
Azerbaijan	10	3	1	6	10	19	-9	10
San Marino	10	0	0	10	2	51	-49	0

Group D

	MP	W	D	L	GF	GA	+/-	Pts
Serbia	10	6	3	1	20	10	10	21
Republic of Ireland	10	5	4	1	12	6	6	19
Wales	10	4	5	1	13	6	7	17
Austria	10	4	3	3	14	12	2	15
Georgia	10	0	5	5	8	14	-6	5
Moldova	10	0	2	8	4	23	-19	2

Group E

	MP	W	D	L	GF	GA	+/-	Pts
Poland	10	8	1	1	28	14	14	25
Denmark	10	6	2	2	20	8	12	20
Montenegro	10	5	1	4	20	12	8	16
Romania	10	3	4	3	12	10	2	13
Armenia	10	2	1	7	10	26	-16	7
Kazakhstan	10	0	3	7	6	26	-20	3

Group F

	MP	W	D	L	GF	GA	+/-	Pts
England	10	8	2	0	18	3	15	26
Slovakia	10	6	0	4	17	7	10	18
Scotland	10	5	3	2	17	12	5	18
Slovenia	10	4	3	3	12	7	5	15
Lithuania	10	1	3	6	7	20	-13	6
Malta	10	0	1	9	3	25	-22	1

Group G

	MP	W	D	L	GF	GA	+/-	Pts
Spain	10	9	1	0	36	3	33	28
Italy	10	7	2	1	21	8	13	23
Albania	10	4	1	5	10	13	-3	13
Israel	10	4	0	6	10	15	-5	12
FYR Macedonia	10	3	2	5	15	15	0	11
Liechtenstein	10	0	0	10	1	39	-38	0

Group H

	MP	W	D	L	GF	GA	+/-	Pts
Belgium	10	9	1	0	43	6	37	28
Greece	10	5	4	1	17	6	11	19
Bosnia and Herzegovina	10	5	2	3	24	13	11	17
Estonia	10	3	2	5	13	19	-6	11
Cyprus	10	3	1	6	9	18	-9	10
Gibraltar	10	0	0	10	3	47	-44	0

Group I

	MP	W	D	L	GF	GA	+/-	Pts
Iceland	10	7	1	2	16	7	9	22
Croatia	10	6	2	2	15	4	11	20
Ukraine	10	5	2	3	13	9	4	17
Turkey	10	4	3	3	14	13	1	15
Finland	10	2	3	5	9	13	-4	9
Kosovo	10	0	1	9	3	24	-21	1

Play-Offs

Northern Ireland 0-1 **Switzerland**
Switzerland 0-0 Northern Ireland 0
Switzerland won 1-0 on aggregate

Denmark 0-0 Republic of Ireland
Republic of Ireland 1-5 **Denmark**
Denmark won 5-1 on aggregate

Sweden 1-0 Italy
Italy 0-0 **Sweden**
Sweden won 1-0 on aggregate

Croatia 4-1 Greece
Greece 0-0 **Croatia**
Croatia won 4-1 on aggregate

QUALIFIED: France, Portugal, Germany, Serbia, Poland, England, Spain, Belgium, Iceland, Switzerland, Denmark, Sweden, Croatia and Russia (hosts)

CONCACAF

	MP	W	D	L	GF	GA	+/-	Pts
Mexico	10	6	3	1	16	7	9	21
Costa Rica	10	4	4	2	14	8	6	16
Panama	10	3	4	3	9	10	-1	13
Honduras	10	3	4	3	13	19	-6	13
USA	10	3	3	4	17	13	4	12
Trinidad & Tobago	10	2	0	8	7	19	-12	6

CONCACAF/Asia Intercontinental Play-Off

Honduras 0-0 **Australia**
Australia 3-1 Honduras
Australia won 3-1 on aggregate

QUALIFIED: Mexico, Costa Rica, Panama

OCEANIA
Round 3

Group A

	MP	W	D	L	GF	GA	+/-	Pts
New Zealand	4	3	1	0	6	0	6	10
New Caledonia	4	1	2	1	4	5	-1	5
Fiji	4	0	1	3	3	8	-5	1

Group B

	MP	W	D	L	GF	GA	+/-	Pts
Solomon Islands	4	3	0	1	6	6	0	9
Tahiti	4	2	0	2	7	4	3	6
Papua New Guinea	4	1	0	3	6	9	-3	3

South America/Oceania Intercontinental Play-Off

New Zealand 0-0 **Peru**
Peru 2-0 New Zealand
Peru won 2-0 on aggregate

BELOW: Christian Eriksen (10) salutes Denmark's travelling fans in Dublin after scoring in the 5-1 win over the Republic of Ireland in the second leg of their European play-off.

THE FINAL DRAW

The 2018 FIFA World Cup Russia™ was served with a perfect call to sporting arms by two heads of their respective states - Vladimir Putin, President of the Russian Federation, and Gianni Infantino, President of FIFA.

The two leaders set the stage for the players and support staffs of the 32 nations who have either fulfilled expectations or, in some cases, even exceeded them in reaching the showpiece event of the world game. They will command the attention of millions of fans around the world for just over one month after the smooth delivery of the draw within a suitably iconic venue, Moscow's State Kremlin Palace.

The Russian hosts will play Saudi Arabia in the opening match at the Luzhniki Stadium in Moscow on 14 June; Egypt and two-time champions Uruguay complete their Group A. Three days later holders Germany will also launch their campaign at the Luzhniki, in their case in Group F against Mexico with Sweden and Korea Republic in waiting. The Luzhniki will also stage the last act of football's grand theatrical experience on Sunday, 15 July.

Matches such as these will further furnish the historic status of the Luzhniki Stadium after a five-year, €300m rebuilding project. Built in 1956, it hosted the Soviet *Spartakiade* extravaganzas, was the centrepiece venue for the 1980 Olympic Games and hosted the 2008 UEFA Champions League Final between Manchester United and Chelsea.

A 25,000-capacity Fan Fest site will sit on the opposite side of the river below the Moscow state university in one of the distinctive so-called "seven sisters".

ABOVE: Football's focus turns to the action on stage at the Final Draw in the State Kremlin Palace in Moscow on 1 December, 2017.

Now for more sporting history in a World Cup already replete with dramatic plot twists in the qualifying competition. Four-times champions Italy, two-time runners-up Netherlands, South American champions Chile and African title-holders Cameroon are all among the absentees from a finals tournament which presents an intriguing balance of competition. Excited expectation will fuel the approach for everyone from the multi-titled likes of Germany and Brazil to newcomers Panama.

President Putin launched the draw by welcoming the football world to an event which he expected to provide "a powerful impetus for developing football in the Russian regions and across the globe". He promised: "We will do everything to make this a major sporting festival and bring closer together this great football family which believes in sport, friendship and fair play - values that do not change with time. They are eternal."

FIFA President Infantino followed up by expressing thanks to Russia for all the work undertaken. He then handed over the draw business to a troupe from among the legends of the game present to witness the action, including three-time winner Pelé.

Miroslav Klose, the all-time leading marksman in the World Cup, brought the FIFA World Cup Trophy onto the

ABOVE: Diego Maradona, Argentina's World Cup-winning captain in 1986, provides a helping hand for old rivals England during the draw in Moscow.

stage, closely followed by the draw assistants. They were Gordon Banks (England), Nikita Simonyan (Russia), Diego Forlán (Uruguay), Diego Maradona (Argentina), Laurent Blanc (France), Cafu (Brazil), Carles Puyol (Spain) and Fabio Cannavaro (Italy). Charged with the duty of master of ceremonies was former England striker Gary Lineker, top scorer in the finals in 1986, assisted by Russian broadcaster Maria Komandnaya.

The 32 finalist nations had been sorted into four pots on the basis of the FIFA/Coca-Cola World Ranking. Only Europe could have two nations in one group. Under Lineker's direction, the assembled team of superstars undertook the essential ritual of sorting the teams into their various balanced groups. Lineker managed the complex process smoothly which included a group-jumping process to ensure that teams from the same confederation did not clash, save in the case of Europe.

Ahead of the draw, Infantino and Vitaly Mutko, Deputy Prime Minister and Chairman of the Local Organising Committee, had spoken of the work undertaken in preparation for the party and of their high expectations for the event in June and July.

Mutko had assured fans, the world's media and the organisations' partners of the efforts undertaken by "millions of people" both behind the scenes and on the ground in developing the venues and supporting infrastructure including training camps, hotels, airports and healthcare facilities.

Visiting fans would benefit from a "Fan ID" system to obviate the need for a visa and provide access for ticket-holders to free rail transport. Both the Fan ID concept and the free rail transport had been in operation for the FIFA Confederations Cup in Russia one year ahead of the finals.

Infantino said: "I'm sure the legacy not only for football but society will be immense thanks to the work that has been put into all this organisation. I am convinced Russia 2018 will be the best World Cup ever."

FIFA WORLD CUP RUSSIA 2018
FINAL DR
GROUP A
RUSSIA
SAUDI ARABIA
EGYPT
URUGUAY
GROUP B
PORTUGAL
SPAIN
MOROCCO
IR IRAN
GROUP C
FRANCE
AUSTRALIA
PERU
DENMARK
GROUP D
ARGENTINA
ICELAND
CROATIA
NIGERIA
GROUP E
BRAZIL
SWITZERLAND
COSTA RICA
SERBIA
GROUP F
GERMANY
MEXICO
SWEDEN
KOREA REPUBLIC
GROUP G
BELGIUM
PANAMA
TUNISIA
ENGLAND
GROUP H
POLAND
SENEGAL
COLOMBIA
JAPAN
FIFA WORLD CUP RUSSIA 2018
FIFA WORLD CUP RUSSIA 2018

Meet the Teams

Outstanding teams from every corner of football planet will seize international attention once the FIFA World Cup™ kicks off in Russia on 14 June in the Luzhniki Stadium in Moscow. Three of the 2014 semi-finalists are back and all with title-winning ambitions, from champions Germany to Argentina and Brazil. But the old powers are sure to face unexpected new challenges – such as the one produced by Costa Rica, quarter-finalists four years ago.

LEFT: A little more than six months before the Opening Ceremony of the 2018 FIFA World Cup Russia, the State Kremlin Palace in Moscow was the venue for the Final Draw when the 32 teams learned their opponents in the first round group stage.

GROUP A

RUSSIA

The long wait by Russian fans to welcome the FIFA World Cup™ will end on 14 June, when their home favourites open the 2018 finals in Moscow's Luzhniki Stadium. It's a major challenge for Stanislav Cherchesov's team.

COACH

STANISLAV CHERCHESOV

Cherchesov, 54, was a fine goalkeeper who played for Russia at the 1994 and 2002 FIFA World Cup finals on his way to winning 39 caps. His club career involved four spells with FC Spartak Moscow and experience abroad with Dynamo Dresden and Tirol Innsbruck. He took up coaching in Austria after retiring and returned to Russia with Spartak in 2007. Cherchesov was appointed manager of Russia in succession to Leonid Slutsky in 2016 after successive club appointments with Spartak, Zhemchuzhina Sochi, Terek Grozny, Amkar Perm, Dynamo Moscow and Legia Warsaw.

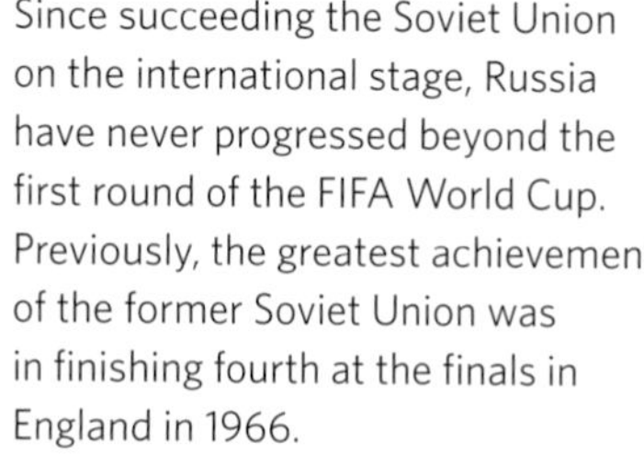

Since succeeding the Soviet Union on the international stage, Russia have never progressed beyond the first round of the FIFA World Cup. Previously, the greatest achievement of the former Soviet Union was in finishing fourth at the finals in England in 1966.

History is with Cherchesov's squad. Only once since the launch of the FIFA World Cup in 1930 has the host nation ever failed to progress beyond the first round group stage. That was in South Africa in 2010.

One of the challenges for a host team is the absence of competitive match action in the run-up to the finals. Coaches of all of the other finalist nations have benefited from the enforced opportunity to hone their player selection and team tactics in the struggle to secure their place in the finals.

Thus last year's FIFA Confederations Cup was an important competitive stepping stone for Russia and for Cherchesov. His work was handicapped by injuries to several senior players. However, the *Sbornaya* opened the tournament in positive fashion with a 2-0 victory over New Zealand in

TASTE OF THINGS TO COME: Russian midfielder Denis Glushakov holds off a challenge from Argentina's central defender Nicolas Otamendi in the opening match of the redeveloped Luzhniki Stadium in Moscow last autumn a match won by Argentina 1-0.

ONES TO WATCH

ALAN DZAGOEV

BORN: 17 June 1990

CLUB: CSKA Moscow

Dzagoev is one of the most outstanding of the latest generation of Russian players. His attacking skills helped CSKA win three league titles, four domestic cups and three Super Cups. He began with Krylia Sovetov and moved to CSKA Moscow in 2008, the year he made his senior national team debut. Dzagoev was joint three-goal top scorer at UEFA EURO 2012.

IGOR AKINFEEV

BORN: 8 April 1986

CLUB: CSKA Moscow

Akinfeev has played more than 100 times for Russia since making his debut in 2004. Subsequently he became captain of his country and played in the 2014 FIFA World Cup and three UEFA European Championships. Akinfeev has won the Russian league title six times and has been a nine-time winner of the Golden Glove Award for Goalkeeper of the Year.

RECORD AT PREVIOUS TOURNAMENTS

As the Soviet Union:

1930-54	did not enter
1958	Quarter-finals
1962	Quarter-finals
1966	4th place
1970	Quarter-finals
1974	did not qualify
1978	did not qualify
1982	2nd round
1986	Round of 16
1990	1st round

As Russia:

1994	1st round
1998	did not qualify
2002	1st round
2006	did not qualify
2010	did not qualify
2014	1st round

front of a supportive capacity crowd in Saint Petersburg.

Russian President Vladimir Putin and FIFA President Gianni Infantino headed a VIP guest list, which included Brazilian legend Pelé. They saw the hosts claim what proved their sole success of the tournament courtesy of a first-half own goal from Michael Boxall and a close-range second-half strike from forward Fyodor Smolov.

Victory was of welcome significance after Russia's elimination in the first round at the finals of the UEFA European Championship in France the previous year.

There, Smolov and attacking right-back Aleksandr Samedov were outstanding against New Zealand. The striker summed up the squad's wider ambition as "wanting to make our supporters and people throughout the country fall in love with the national team during this Confederations Cup".

The Russian team's second outing, however, brought a narrow 1-0 defeat by European champions Portugal in a game that saw captain Igor Akinfeev make his 100th international appearance in goal. Hopes of reaching the semi-finals were then extinguished by Mexico in Kazan. Russia lost 2-1, despite taking an early lead through Samedov.

Cherchesov, reviewing the campaign, said that he was proud of his recast team "for doing as much as they could in the circumstances", which included the need to rely on an internationally inexperienced trio in central defence in Georgy Dzhikiya, Viktor Vasin and Fyodor Kudryashov.

Looking ahead, he said: "I hope all the players will use the experience to grow and develop. I think they have won hearts and minds among our fans and given reasons for confidence going forward. I don't think any of our fans could have any doubts that the team played their hearts out. We managed to play some good football right from the start so that showed we are making steps in the right direction.

"What remains in preparing for the World Cup is to continue to work as we have been and connect the sporting dots."

GROUP A

SAUDI ARABIA

Saudi Arabia's status as one of the most powerful nations in Asian football has been underlined by their return. After missing out in 2010 and 2014, they have a point to prove as three-time past AFC champions.

COACH

JUAN ANTONIO PIZZI

Juan Antonio Pizzi took over as manager of Saudi Arabia after the end of the successful qualifying tournament. The 49-year-old succeeded fellow Argentinian Edgardo Bauza, who had taken over months earlier from Dutchman Bert van Marwijk. Pizzi had played centre-forward for Spain in the 1990s, scoring eight goals in 22 matches. He then coached clubs back in Argentina, Chile, Spain and Mexico before being appointed manager of Chile in 2016. He guided them to victory in the centenary *Copa América* in 2016 and to the final of the FIFA Confederations Cup in Russia last year.

The Saudi FA was founded in 1959 and the national team celebrated initial honours by winning the 1984 and 1988 Asian titles. They maintained the good work by investing heavily in foreign coaching expertise and building the King Fahd International Stadium in Riyadh, which hosted the inaugural FIFA Confederations Cup (then known as the King Fahd Cup) in 1992.

That commitment to the game paid off in another Asian title in 1996 amid a hat-trick of appearances at the FIFA World Cup finals in 1994, 1998 and 2002.

In 1994, under Argentinian coach Jorge Solari, Saudi Arabia beat Belgium and Morocco in the first round before losing to Sweden in the round of 16. The 1-0 win over Belgium was achieved with one of the most brilliant goals in FIFA World Cup history by Saeed Al-Owairan, advancing from within his own half.

In 2002, Saudi Arabia were defeated 8-0 by Germany in their first group game and exited the tournament after failing to pick up either a point or a goal. The Saudi FA promised a major overhaul of the domestic game, and their efforts have

MEN ON A MISSION: Saudi Arabia, captained by Osama Hawsawi (back row, far right), line up before their 1-0 victory over Japan in the King Abdullah Sports City in Jeddah which secured their return to the FIFA World Cup finals for the first time since 2006.

ONES TO WATCH

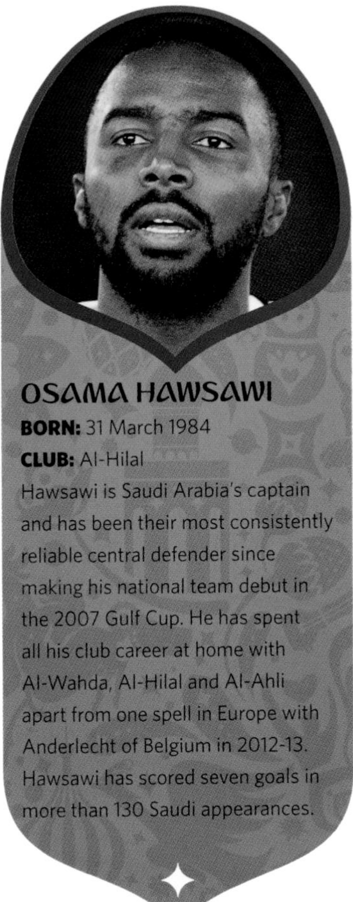

OSAMA HAWSAWI

BORN: 31 March 1984
CLUB: Al-Hilal
Hawsawi is Saudi Arabia's captain and has been their most consistently reliable central defender since making his national team debut in the 2007 Gulf Cup. He has spent all his club career at home with Al-Wahda, Al-Hilal and Al-Ahli apart from one spell in Europe with Anderlecht of Belgium in 2012-13. Hawsawi has scored seven goals in more than 130 Saudi appearances.

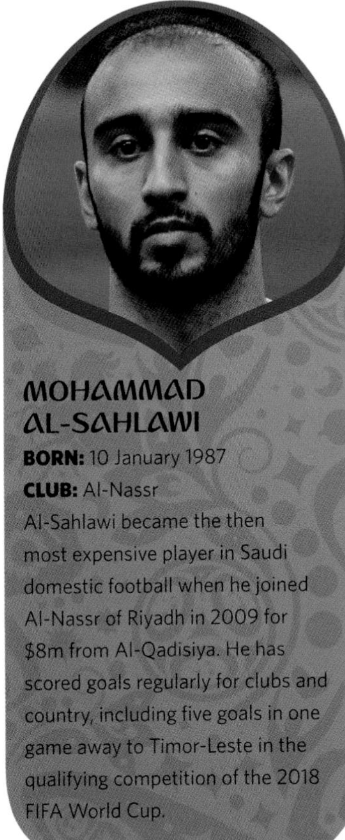

MOHAMMAD AL-SAHLAWI

BORN: 10 January 1987
CLUB: Al-Nassr
Al-Sahlawi became the then most expensive player in Saudi domestic football when he joined Al-Nassr of Riyadh in 2009 for $8m from Al-Qadisiya. He has scored goals regularly for clubs and country, including five goals in one game away to Timor-Leste in the qualifying competition of the 2018 FIFA World Cup.

RECORD AT PREVIOUS TOURNAMENTS

Year	Record
1930	did not exist
1934	not in membership
1938	not in membership
1950	not in membership
1954	not in membership
1958	not in membership
1962	did not enter
1966	did not enter
1970	did not enter
1974	did not enter
1978	did not qualify
1982	did not qualify
1986	did not qualify
1990	did not qualify
1994	Round of 16
1998	1st round
2002	1st round
2006	1st round
2010	did not qualify
2014	did not qualify

been rewarded with their return to the finals.

Saudi history includes some of the most iconic players in the Asian game, including Mohamed Al-Deayea and Majed Abdullah. Al-Deayea kept goal in four FIFA World Cups and, between 1993 and 2006, made 178 appearances, a world record for a goalkeeper.

At the other end of the pitch, Saudi Arabia were inspired for years by Abdullah, the so-called "Desert Pelé". Abdullah ranks among the greatest marksmen in national team football history after scoring 115 goals for his country during an era in which he was voted Asian Footballer of the Year on three occasions.

The baton has been passed to successors such as goalkeeper Waleed Abdullah, captain Osama Hawsawi, fellow defensive stalwart Hassan Muath, midfielders Taisir Al-Jassim and Yahya Al-Shehri plus striker Mohammad Al-Sahlawi. Both Hawsawi and Al-Jassim have played more than a 120 internationals since making their national team debuts 11 years ago.

Saudi Arabia were seeded directly to the second round of the Asian qualifying competition, where they topped Group A ahead of the United Arab Emirates, Palestine, Malaysia and Timor-Leste.

Dutch coach Bert van Marwijk saw his Saudi team top the table with six wins and two draws and a commanding goal difference of 28-4. The match in Malaysia was abandoned near the end because of objects thrown onto the pitch. The Saudis, 2-1 ahead at the time, were awarded the game 3-0 by FIFA.

Some 17 of Saudi's goals came in two ties against Timor-Leste. Al-Sahlawi scored a hat-trick in a 7-0 win at home in Jeddah and five in the 10-0 away victory in Dili. He was the round's leading marksman with 14 goals, followed by Al-Shehri with three.

In the third round, the Saudis qualified for the finals by virtue of finishing runners-up to Japan in Group B, edging Australia on goal difference. A 1-0 win over Japan on the last matchday, through a second-half strike from Fahad Al-Muwallad, proved decisive as, simultaneously, the Australians managed to defeat Thailand by only 2-1 and thus failed to edge up into second spot.

GROUP A

EGYPT

Egypt have waited a very long time to reclaim their place at the apex of the FIFA World Cup™. In fact, this will be the *Pharaohs'* first appearance in the finals since Italy in 1990.

COACH

HÉCTOR CÚPER

Cúper, 62, is one of the most experienced and widely travelled coaches at the FIFA World Cup. The Argentinian was twice a national championship winner as a central defender with Ferro Carril Oeste. He moved to Huracán before becoming coach and moving to European football with Real Mallorca. Further appointments followed in Spain, Italy and Greece before Cúper progressed to national team football, initially with Georgia and then, in 2015, Egypt. Cúper took the team to the runners-up slot at the 2017 Africa Cup of Nations before achieving qualification for Russia.

On that occasion, their campaign ended behind England, the Republic of Ireland and the Netherlands in a highly competitive first-round group played out in Sardinia and Sicily. A team coached by Mahmoud El-Gohary drew with both the Dutch and Irish before losing by a single goal to eventual semi-finalists England.

Egypt boasts a long, proud history in the regional and international game. The Egyptian Football Association was founded in 1921 and became the first African nation to join FIFA in 1923. They were also one of the four founder members of the Confédération Africaine de Football on its creation in 1957.

They could already point to international achievement. Egypt had finished fourth in the football tournament at the 1928 Summer Olympics in Amsterdam and entered the FIFA World Cup for the first time in 1934, when they defeated Palestine in a qualifying play-off before losing 4-2 to Hungary in the first round of the finals in Italy.

Egypt won the inaugural Africa Cup of Nations, in Sudan in 1957, and the second edition, as hosts,

BACK IN THE FINALS ACTION: Egyptian forward Mohamed Salah outpaces Congo's Tobias Badila during their African zone qualifying match in Alexandria last October. Salah scored both Egypt's goals in a 2-1 victory, the winner coming in additional time, to seal the Pharoahs' berths on the plane to Russia.

ONES TO WATCH

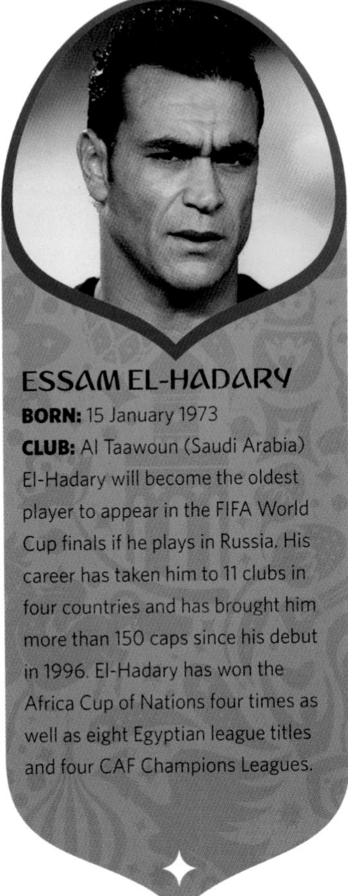

ESSAM EL-HADARY

BORN: 15 January 1973

CLUB: Al Taawoun (Saudi Arabia)

El-Hadary will become the oldest player to appear in the FIFA World Cup finals if he plays in Russia. His career has taken him to 11 clubs in four countries and has brought him more than 150 caps since his debut in 1996. El-Hadary has won the Africa Cup of Nations four times as well as eight Egyptian league titles and four CAF Champions Leagues.

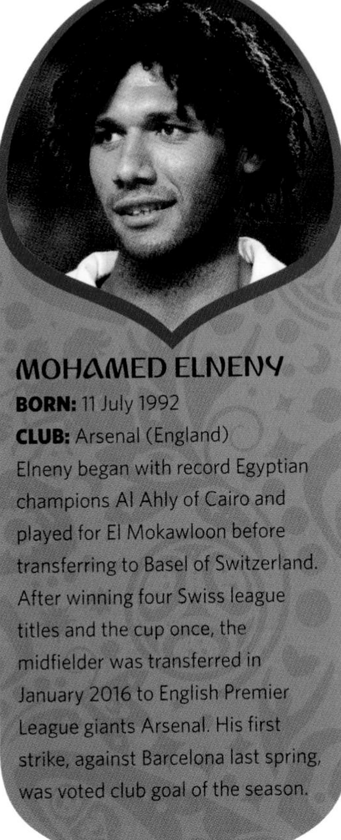

MOHAMED ELNENY

BORN: 11 July 1992

CLUB: Arsenal (England)

Elneny began with record Egyptian champions Al Ahly of Cairo and played for El Mokawloon before transferring to Basel of Switzerland. After winning four Swiss league titles and the cup once, the midfielder was transferred in January 2016 to English Premier League giants Arsenal. His first strike, against Barcelona last spring, was voted club goal of the season.

RECORD AT PREVIOUS TOURNAMENTS

1930	did not enter
1934	1st round
1938	withdrew
1950	did not enter
1954	did not qualify
1958	withdrew
1962	withdrew
1966	withdrew
1970	did not enter
1974	did not qualify
1978	did not qualify
1982	did not qualify
1986	did not qualify
1990	1st round
1994	did not qualify
1998	did not qualify
2002	did not qualify
2006	did not qualify
2010	did not qualify
2014	did not qualify

two years later. They were Olympic semi-finalists again in 1964, finished third in the Cup of Nations in 1970 and 1974, finished fourth in 1976 and reached the Olympic quarter-finals in 1984. Down all these years, and for various reasons, Egypt remained absent from the grand stage of the FIFA World Cup finals, but finally brought a 56-year absence to an end in 1990.

A further absence of 24 years then followed, during which, even so, Egypt won the Cup of Nations on a further four occasions to reach their current record of seven successes.

Two domestic clubs have similar international success: Al Ahly have won 20 international competitions as well as a record 39 national championships and 36 cups while old rivals Zamalek boast 11 Afro-Asian titles plus 12 league crowns and 25 domestic cups.

Egypt's latest attempt to end their luckless pursuit of FIFA World Cup qualification began with a second-round direct elimination tie against Chad. They lost the away leg 1-0 but turned the tie around with a 4-0 home victory in the second leg in Alexandria. Mohamed Elneny struck the opening goal after only five minutes to point Egypt towards the finals. Abdallah Said scored the second with Hassan Mahgoub, from Portugal's SC Braga, claiming two more.

Victory propelled Egypt into the third round, comprising five groups whose winners would qualify for the finals. Egypt were in Group E with Uganda, Ghana and Congo and made the perfect start with a 2-1 win away to Congo, thanks to goals from star striker Mo Salah and Said again. The same pair struck again to provide a follow-up 2-0 home win over Ghana.

Salah struck two more goals in the 2-1 home win over Congo, which secured Egypt's place in the finals with one round of matches still to play. Finally the *Pharaohs* were back in the FIFA World Cup finals, a special achievement for ecstatic home fans following various difficulties within the domestic game.

Supporters had been barred from attending domestic league matches after crowd problems including the Port Said tragedy in which 74 people died in 2012.

GROUP A URUGUAY

Uruguay are one of the greatest nations in FIFA World Cup™ history, feared for an ability to raise their game on the greatest stage. As two-time champions the *Celeste* will be dangerous rivals for anyone in Russia.

COACH

ÓSCAR WASHINGTON TABÁREZ

Tabárez, 71, is one of the world's longest-serving national managers after 12 years in this second spell in the Uruguayan job. These years have included two awards as South American Coach of the Year, victory in the 2011 *Copa América* and fourth place at the FIFA World Cup in 2010. A teacher, Tabárez was a defender who played his club football in Uruguay and Mexico, and then coached top clubs in Colombia, Italy and Argentina. Tabárez holds a South American managerial record: 60 matches in FIFA World Cup qualifying competitions. He is also the fifth-ranked manager, with 26 games in five editions of the *Copa América*.

Luis Suárez and Edinson Cavani are two of the most outstanding strikers in international football, and have considerable FIFA World Cup experience and more than 90 goals between them at national-team level. They combined for 15 of Uruguay's 32 goals in the South American qualifying campaign to extend their small country's great footballing heritage.

Uruguay dominated world football in the first half of the twentieth century. Early successes in the South American Championship were followed by victory in the 1924 Summer Olympics in Amsterdam. Uruguay repeated the success in Paris in 1928 and then two years later, as the host nation, swept to victory in the first FIFA World Cup.

The side of the 1920s and 1930s contained many of Uruguay's all-time greats: skipper José Nasazzi, the half-backs José Andrade, Lorenzo Fernández and Álvaro Gestido, and outstanding forwards in Héctor Castro, José Pedro Cea and Héctor Scarone.

In 1950, Uruguay reclaimed their status on top of the world by defeating hosts Brazil 2-1 in the

ON THE ROAD TO RUSSIA: Delighted Federico Valverde (second left) celebrates with team-mates, from left to right, Luis Suárez, José Maria Jimenez, Carlos Sanchez, Matias Vecino and Cristhian Stuani, after scoring Uruguay's first goal against Paraguay in Asuncion. The Celeste qualified with two rounds of the qualifying competition to go.

ONES TO WATCH

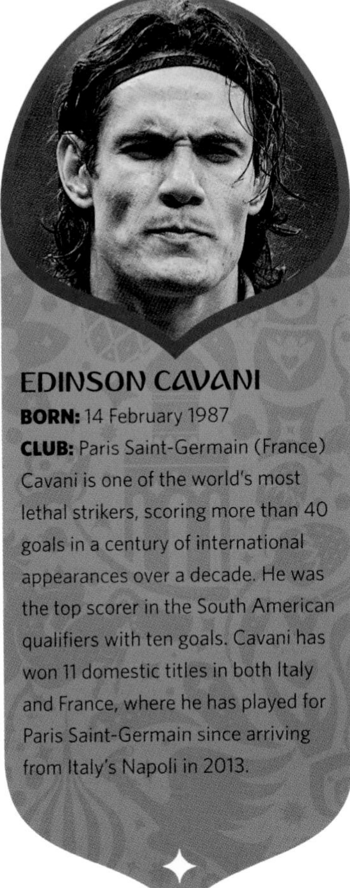

EDINSON CAVANI

BORN: 14 February 1987
CLUB: Paris Saint-Germain (France)
Cavani is one of the world's most lethal strikers, scoring more than 40 goals in a century of international appearances over a decade. He was the top scorer in the South American qualifiers with ten goals. Cavani has won 11 domestic titles in both Italy and France, where he has played for Paris Saint-Germain since arriving from Italy's Napoli in 2013.

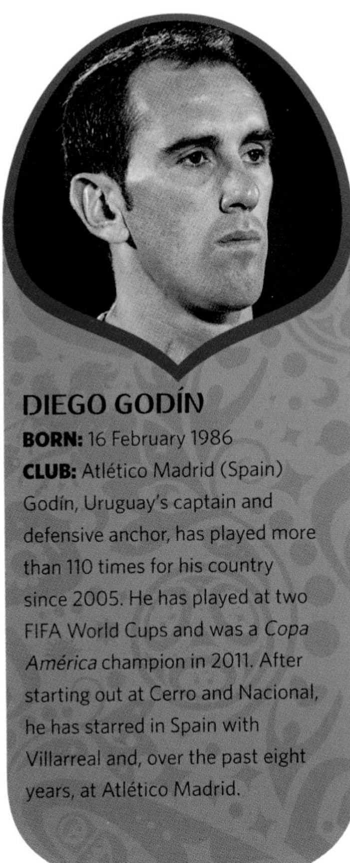

DIEGO GODÍN

BORN: 16 February 1986
CLUB: Atlético Madrid (Spain)
Godín, Uruguay's captain and defensive anchor, has played more than 110 times for his country since 2005. He has played at two FIFA World Cups and was a *Copa América* champion in 2011. After starting out at Cerro and Nacional, he has starred in Spain with Villarreal and, over the past eight years, at Atlético Madrid.

RECORD AT PREVIOUS TOURNAMENTS

1930	CHAMPIONS
1934	did not enter
1938	did not enter
1950	CHAMPIONS
1954	4th place
1958	did not qualify
1962	1st round
1966	Quarter-finals
1970	4th place
1974	1st round
1978	did not qualify
1982	did not qualify
1986	Round of 16
1990	Round of 16
1994	did not qualify
1998	did not qualify
2002	1st round
2006	did not qualify
2010	4th place
2014	Round of 16

final in Rio de Janeiro's Maracaña Stadium. Now their inspirations were inside forward Juan Schiaffino, wing-half Victor Andrade, captain and centre-half Obdulio Varela plus match-winner Alcides Ghiggia at outside right.

They finished fourth in 1954 and 1970, but subsequent FIFA World Cups proved largely disappointing despite the efforts of star forwards such as Fernando Morena and Enzo Francescoli. Finally, in 2010, the inspiration of Suárez and Diego Forlán lifted Uruguay back into the last four for the first time in 40 years. They followed that up by winning the *Copa América*, in 2011, for a record 15th time.

In the old days, Uruguay's squad was built around the players of Montevideo's two great clubs, Club Atlético Peñarol and Nacional, who have dominated the domestic game and collected a host of international trophies. Now, coach Oscar Washington Tabárez can draw his squad from a wide range of clubs in Argentina, Brazil, France, Italy, Mexico, the Netherlands, Portugal and Spain.

They boast vast experience, with several players boasting a century or more of international caps – including goalkeeper Fernando Muslera, defenders such as captain Diego Godín and Maxi Pereira, midfielder Cristian Rodríguez and strikers Cavani and Suárez.

The South American qualifying tournament involved all ten members of the regional confederation, CONMEBOL. Uruguay got off to a positive start with a run of victories over Bolivia, Colombia and Chile punctuated by defeat in Ecuador. Impressively, goals from Cavani and Suárez secured a 2-2 draw away to Brazil before Cavani struck the lone-goal winner at home to Peru.

Defeat in Argentina preceded victories over Paraguay and Venezuela, but then came three successive defeats away to Chile, home to Brazil and away to Peru, which left the *Celeste* in danger of not making it to Russia. Home to Bolivia, they regained winning form just when it mattered most. Goals from Martín Cáceres, Cavani and Suárez (two) saw Uruguay finish as group runners-up to Brazil and safely on their way to Russia.

GROUP B

PORTUGAL

European champions Portugal approach Russia 2018 with the ambition of achieving the same double as Iberian neighbours Spain in 2010. As ever, they will depend on the inspirational leadership of Cristiano Ronaldo.

COACH

FERNANDO SANTOS

Santos, 63, is pursuing a double after steering Portugal to victory at UEFA EURO 2016. He never played high-level football but proved outstanding as a coach with FC Porto, AEK, Panathinaikos and PAOK in Greece as well as with local rivals Sporting Lisbon and Benfica. In 2010 he turned to national-team football with Greece. He led them to the quarter-finals of UEFA EURO 2012, then to the second round of the 2014 FIFA World Cup. Two months later he succeeded Paulo Bento as Portugal's coach and led them to glory in France.

The Real Madrid striker spearheads a squad mixing title-winning experience with a new generation of youngsters whose talents have drawn comparisons with the so-called "golden generation" of Luís Figo, Rui Costa and Paulo Sousa, who won FIFA world youth crowns in 1989 and 1991.

Portugal had to wait for their first major senior success until the 2016 UEFA European Championship, when they defeated hosts France 1-0 after extra time in Saint-Denis. Victory, achieved with a goal from France-based striker Eder, was a long-overdue reward for Portugal's contribution to the world game.

The Portuguese FA was founded in 1914 by a merger of the associations of Lisbon and Oporto. The first statements at international level were made by record league title-winners Benfica, winning the UEFA European Champions Cup twice (1961 and 1962) and reaching three more finals.

Benfica also provided the bulk of the national team who finished third at the 1966 FIFA World Cup in England. Until Cristiano

TOPPING THE TABLE IN STYLE: Portugal's forward Andre Silva celebrates his goal, the second in a 2-0 victory over Switzerland in Lisbon last October, a result which helped secure top spot in European Group B and a guaranteed place in the finals.

ONES TO WATCH

NANI
(Luís Carlos Almeida da Cunha)

BORN: 17 November 1986
CLUB: Lazio (Italy)
Nani was one of the stars of the European title-winning team, playing on both wings and occasionally at centre-forward. He has claimed more than 100 caps since his goalscoring debut against Denmark in 2006. Nani has won more than a dozen trophies in a club career with Sporting Lisbon, Manchester United, Fenerbahçe, Valencia and Lazio.

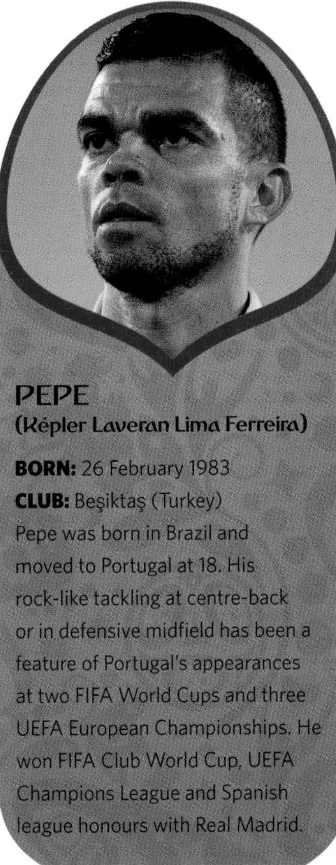

PEPE
(Képler Laveran Lima Ferreira)

BORN: 26 February 1983
CLUB: Beşiktaş (Turkey)
Pepe was born in Brazil and moved to Portugal at 18. His rock-like tackling at centre-back or in defensive midfield has been a feature of Portugal's appearances at two FIFA World Cups and three UEFA European Championships. He won FIFA Club World Cup, UEFA Champions League and Spanish league honours with Real Madrid.

RECORD AT PREVIOUS TOURNAMENTS

1930	did not enter
1934	did not qualify
1938	did not qualify
1950	did not qualify
1954	did not qualify
1958	did not qualify
1962	did not qualify
1966	3rd place
1970	did not qualify
1974	did not qualify
1978	did not qualify
1982	did not qualify
1986	Round of 16
1990	did not qualify
1994	did not qualify
1998	did not qualify
2002	1st round
2006	4th place
2010	Round of 16
2014	1st round

Ronaldo came along, their hero was Mozambique-born striker Eusébio, who was the 1966 finals' nine-goal leading scorer.

Playmaker Mário Coluna, also from Mozambique, was another product of the then Portuguese colonies in an impressive side that included Benfica wingers José Augusto and António Simões and centre-forward José Torres.

After a "lost decade" in the 1970s, Portugal revived in the 1980s as Porto won the Champions Cup and Benfica reached the finals of both the Champions Cup and UEFA Cup. Portugal's youngsters won two FIFA age-group crowns in 1989 and 1991 and star graduate Figo would later be crowned both world and European Player of the Year.

Porto, under José Mourinho, won the UEFA Cup and Champions League in 2003 and 2004 to spark a renewal of confidence in the national team, who duly finished runners-up as hosts at UEFA EURO 2004 and then took fourth place at the 2006 FIFA World Cup.

The then new starlet Cristiano Ronaldo has subsequently grown up into one of the game's greatest players, a Portuguese record holder of both caps and goals as well as the captain who lifted the European trophy at UEFA EURO 2016.

Two months later, Ronaldo was absent through injury as title-winning team-mates such as goalkeeper Rui Patrício, defenders Pepe, Cédric and José Fonte, midfielders João Moutinho, William Silva de Carvalho, Adrien Silva and forward Nani opened Portugal's FIFA World Cup qualifying campaign with a 2-0 defeat in Switzerland.

That proved to be Portugal's only defeat. Both nations won all their eight subsequent Group B games before meeting again at the Estádio da Luz in Lisbon on the last matchday. Portugal turned the tables. They won 2-0 to pull level with the Swiss on 27 points and ahead on goal difference.

On this occasion Ronaldo, the group's 15-goal leading scorer, did not find the net. Instead, an own goal from Johan Djourou and a strike from Adrien Silva took Portugal to the finals for the fifth successive time and the seventh time in their history.

GROUP B

SPAIN

Spain set a new European standard with their historic hat-trick of one FIFA World Cup™ and two European crowns between 2008 and 2012. They were deposed as world champions in Brazil and bring a rebuilt team to Russia.

COACH

JULEN LOPETEGUI

Lopetegui, 51, is a former national team goalkeeper. He played 149 league games over 11 years for Real Madrid, Logroñés, Barcelona and Rayo Vallecano. He was a member of Spain's squad at the 1994 FIFA World Cup. In 2003, he moved into coaching on the Spanish FA youth staff. After spells with Rayo and Real Madrid B, Lopetegui returned to the Spanish FA in 2010 and led the U-19s and U-21s to victories in their UEFA European competitions. After two seasons with FC Porto, he was appointed successor as Spain coach to Vicente del Bosque.

For years, the reputation of Spanish football was dependent on the achievements of Real Madrid and Barcelona. The success of *La Roja* in winning the UEFA European Championship in 2008 was long overdue as Spain had gone 44 years without anything to celebrate. Victory in Vienna proved a launch pad towards grander achievements: the FIFA World Cup triumph in 2010 and a UEFA European Championship repeat in 2012.

Football gained a foothold in the Basque country of Northern Spain through migrant British workers in the 1890s, and the Spanish FA was founded in 1913.

The national side made their debut at the 1920 Summer Olympics and went on to reach the quarter-finals of the 1928 Olympics and the 1934 FIFA World Cup. Each time, a team starring the great goalkeeper Ricardo Zamora lost to Italy.

The Spanish Civil War and Second World War halted national team competition for almost a decade and Spain were absent from the international headlines until they won the UEFA European Nations' Cup as hosts in 1964. A side guided

THE GOAL THAT CHEERS: Spanish forward Isco (No. 22) is mobbed by thrilled team-mates, including Sergio Ramos (left) and Jordi Alba (18) after scoring the first of his two goals in a 3-0 victory over Italy in their European qualifying tie in Madrid last September.

ONES TO WATCH

DAVID DE GEA

BORN: 7 November 1990

CLUB: Manchester United (England)

De Gea made his name with Atlético Madrid before raising his game with Manchester United in the English Premier League since 2011. He captained Spain to victory in the UEFA U-21 European Championship in both 2011 and 2013, and also played at the 2012 Summer Olympics. He made his senior debut in 2014 and subsequently succeeded Iker Casillas as goalkeeper for the national team.

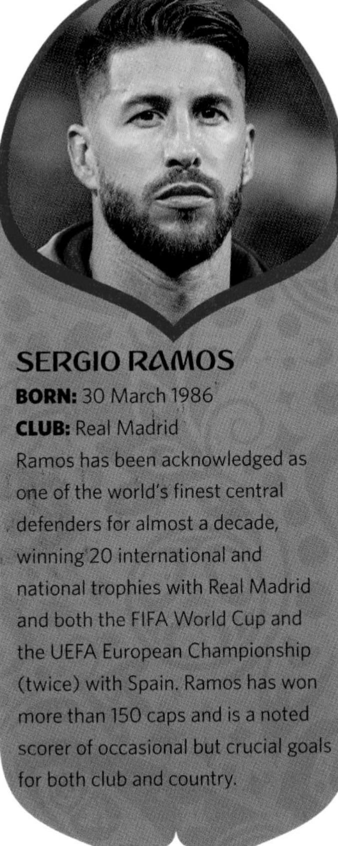

SERGIO RAMOS

BORN: 30 March 1986

CLUB: Real Madrid

Ramos has been acknowledged as one of the world's finest central defenders for almost a decade, winning 20 international and national trophies with Real Madrid and both the FIFA World Cup and the UEFA European Championship (twice) with Spain. Ramos has won more than 150 caps and is a noted scorer of occasional but crucial goals for both club and country.

RECORD AT PREVIOUS TOURNAMENTS

1930	did not enter
1934	Quarter-finals
1938	withdrew
1950	4th place
1954	did not qualify
1958	did not qualify
1962	1st round
1966	1st round
1970	did not qualify
1974	did not qualify
1978	1st round
1982	2nd round
1986	Quarter-finals
1990	1st round
1994	Quarter-finals
1998	1st round
2002	Quarter-finals
2006	Round of 16
2010	CHAMPIONS
2014	1st round

by Luis "Luisito" Suárez, among the greatest of Spanish playmakers, beat the Soviet Union 2-1 in Madrid to clinch Spain's first major trophy.

Over the next 30 years, the best Spain achieved was finishing as European runners-up in 1984 and reaching the FIFA World Cup quarter-finals in 1986. Finally a breakthrough was achieved in 1992. Gold-medal success at the Summer Olympics in Barcelona was followed by the rise of superb home-grown players from Barcelona, such as playmakers Xavi and Andrés Iniesta.

These, along with other club-mates including the Madrid stars Iker Casillas (goalkeeper-captain) and Sergio Ramos (defender), provided the nucleus of a national team that reached historic heights. Between November 2006 and June 2009, Spain were unbeaten for a record-equalling 35 games.

Fernando Torres scored the goal that beat Germany in the 2008 European final and one of the four that left Italy outclassed in 2012. Iniesta was named best player at the 2010 FIFA World Cup in South Africa, enhancing a reputation established with his extra-time winner in the FIFA World Cup Final victory over the Netherlands.

Coach Julen Lopetegui, who succeeded Vicente del Bosque after the FIFA World Cup loss in 2014, has rebuilt the team. David de Gea took over in goal from Iker Casillas, but Sergio Ramos, Gerard Piqué and Jordi Alba still provide a solid core in defence. In midfield Sergio Busquets and Andrés Iniesta have won more than 100 caps, as has David Silva, a worthy successor to Xavi.

Lopetegui has experimented with different attacking options, including experienced Pedro as well as Diego Costa and his Chelsea successor Álvaro Morata. Costa, Morata, Silva and Real Madrid's Isco scored five goals apiece as Spain qualified for Russia. They won nine games, drew one and lost none, scoring 36 goals and conceding a mere three.

The only match in which they dropped points was a 1-1 draw away to fellow former world champions Italy in October 2016. They made no mistake in the return, winning 3-0 at the Estadio Santiago Bernabéu to stamp their command on European qualifying.

GROUP B

MOROCCO

Morocco are back in the FIFA World Cup™ finals for the first time since 1998. The work of coach Hervé Renard has paid off with progress to the quarter-finals of the Africa Cup of Nations last year and now by reaching Russia.

COACH

HERVÉ RENARD

Renard, 49, is a French coach who has made his name with African national teams. As a youngster, he played for AS Cannes alongside Zinédine Zidane. He worked briefly in management in China, England (for Cambridge United), Vietnam and France before becoming coach of Zambia in 2008. In 2012, he guided Zambia to victory in the Africa Cup of Nations, and in 2015 he did the same for Côte d'Ivoire, becoming the first coach to win the African crown with different nations. He took over Morocco's *Atlas Lions* in early 2016 from Ezzaki "Zaki" Badou.

The *Atlas Lions* first appeared on the global stage at the FIFA World Cup finals in Mexico in 1970. Their second adventure was also in Mexico, in 1986, when they topped a first-round group featuring England and Portugal before losing 1-0 to West Germany in the round of 16.

Two further appearances at the finals followed: in 1994 and 1998. On the latter occasion, Morocco thought they had reached the round of 16 after a 3-0 victory over Scotland. Mustapha Hadji and his team-mates were already celebrating on the pitch when they learned that Norway had beaten Brazil to snatch second spot from them.

Now Morocco have finally re-emerged from the sidelines courtesy of a long-awaited new generation that includes defenders Medhi Benatia and Nabil Dirar, midfielders Moubarak "Mbark" Boussoufa and Noureddine "Nordin" Amrabat plus forward Youssef El-Arabi.

In the qualifying competition, the Moroccans were seeded directly to the second round, where they defeated Equatorial Guinea 2-1 on aggregate in November 2015. They

FLYING HIGH OUT OF AFRICA: Morocco's Boutaib Khalid salutes the crowd after scoring one of his three goals against Gabon last October in the African FIFA World Cup qualifying competition at the Mohammed V Stadium in Casablanca.

ONES TO WATCH

MEDHI BENATIA

BORN: 17 April 1987
CLUB: Juventus (Italy)

Benatia, Moroccan captain and central defender, debuted for Morocco in 2008 and was appointed captain in 2013. Born in France, he played for Marseille, FC Tours and Clermont before moving to Italy to play for Udinese and Roma. He then won the German league and cup with Bayern Munich before returning to Italy on loan with Juventus.

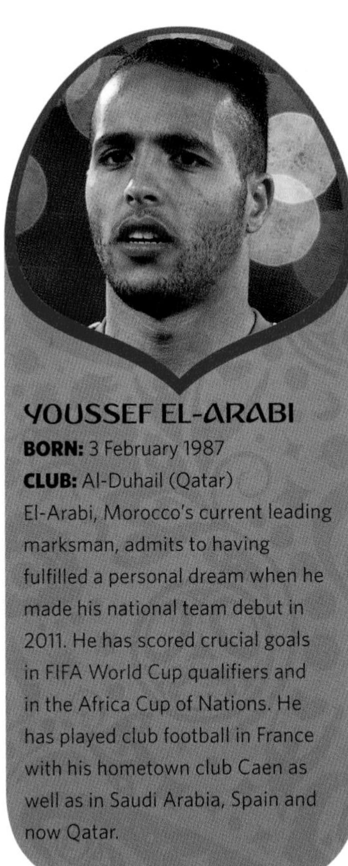

YOUSSEF EL-ARABI

BORN: 3 February 1987
CLUB: Al-Duhail (Qatar)

El-Arabi, Morocco's current leading marksman, admits to having fulfilled a personal dream when he made his national team debut in 2011. He has scored crucial goals in FIFA World Cup qualifiers and in the Africa Cup of Nations. He has played club football in France with his hometown club Caen as well as in Saudi Arabia, Spain and now Qatar.

RECORD AT PREVIOUS TOURNAMENTS

1930	did not exist
1934	did not exist
1938	did not exist
1950	did not exist
1954	did not exist
1958	did not enter
1962	did not qualify
1966	withdrew
1970	1st round
1974	did not qualify
1978	did not qualify
1982	did not qualify
1986	Round of 16
1990	did not qualify
1994	1st round
1998	1st round
2002	did not qualify
2006	did not qualify
2010	did not qualify
2014	did not qualify

won 2-0 at home with goals from El-Arabi and Yacine Bammou and lost 1-0 away to reach the third round Group C with Gabon, Côte d'Ivoire and Mali.

By the time Morocco returned to action, Frenchman Hervé Renard had taken over as national team coach. Initially they were challenged in attack, being held to goalless draws in three of their first four games, away to Gabon and Mali as well as at home to Côte d'Ivoire . In between, they scored six against a Mali side who finished bottom of the group without winning a game. Hakim Ziyech, the Ajax midfielder, scored twice including a penalty.

Khalid Boutaïb scored Morocco's only hat-trick of the competition, all three goals in a 3-0 win over Gabon, which put them in pole position ahead of the concluding matchday.

In Abidjan, hosts Côte d'Ivoire needed to beat Morocco to finish top of the group. For Morocco, a draw would have been enough. Even better, they took early command when a left-footed, right-wing cross from Nabil Dirar eluded Ivorian goalkeeper Sylvain Gbohouo to provide a 25th-minute lead. Five minutes later, the Ivorians hesitated at a corner and skipper Medhi Benatia jabbed the ball home for a 2-0 win and a place in the finals in Russia in June.

The Moroccan FA was founded after independence from France was attained in 1956. Morocco joined FIFA in 1960 and the Confederation of African Football (CAF) in 1966. Before then, however, Morocco had provided a stream of outstanding players to the French, including Larbi Benbarek, the so-called "Black Pearl", and later the Marrakech-born Just Fontaine, who scored a record 13 goals for France in the 1958 FIFA World Cup finals.

The national team have won the Africa Cup of Nations once, in 1976, while club success at international level has included three victories in the CAF Champions League for Raja Casablanca, two for neighbours Wydad - including the 2017 title - and one for ASFAR.

Wydad achieved the added bonus of reaching the FIFA Club World Cup with their 2-1 aggregate win over Egypt's Al Ahly in the most high-profile African club competition.

GROUP B

IR IRAN

IR Iran fly to the finals for the fifth time, more determined than ever to reach the knockout stage for the first time. They look to the FIFA World Cup™ experience of stars such as goalkeeper Alireza Haghighu and forward Ashkan Dejagah.

COACH

CARLOS QUEIROZ

Queiroz, 65, holds a record as IR Iran's longest-serving national team coach: having started work in 2011, he led them to the FIFA World Cup finals in 2014. Born in Portuguese Mozambique, he entered the international arena in the late 1980s as coach of Portugal's double world youth champions. Queiroz took over the seniors in 1991. Later he coached South Africa and returned there with Portugal for the 2010 FIFA World Cup. Club appointments have included Sporting Lisbon, Real Madrid and assistant manager at Manchester United.

Coach Carlos Queiroz's team had been seeded directly into the second round of the Asian qualifying section, where they were drawn in Group D along with Oman, Turkmenistan, Guam and India. They opened with a 1-1 draw in Turkmenistan, then defeated Guam 6-0. Striker Sardar Azmoun scored IR Iran's point-winning goal away in Dasoguz and then two more at home to Guam.

The Iranians also won 3-0 away to India next time out with Azmoun again on the scoresheet. In the event FIFA awarded IR Iran a 3-0 win because India had fielded midfielder Eugeneson Lyngdoh despite his suspension after yellow cards in two previous games.

IR Iran finished the group undefeated in their eight games to reach a third qualifying mini-league with China PR, Korea Republic, Qatar, Syria and Uzbekistan. Again they were unbeaten both home and away. They scored only ten goals but, crucially, conceded only two.

The most important duels were with Korea Republic, experienced FIFA World Cup campaigners. The Iranians won 1-0 in Tehran in front of 75,800 fans with a first-half goal

TARGET MAN AT THE DOUBLE: Sardar Azmoun of IR Iran enjoys the moment after striking one his two goals against Syria in Tehran, in their final game of their Asian qualifying group. Ultimately, however, Azmoun and his team-mates were held to a 2-2 draw in the Azadi Stadium.

ONES TO WATCH

ASHKAN DEJAGAH

BORN: 5 June 1986

CLUB: VfL Wolfsburg (Germany)

Dejagah was born in Tehran but moved to Berlin when he was one and played for Germany at youth levels. He won the 2009 UEFA European U-21 title before deciding to play senior football for IR Iran. He has won more than 40 caps since his debut in 2012, including all three of their matches at the FIFA World Cup finals in Brazil in 2014.

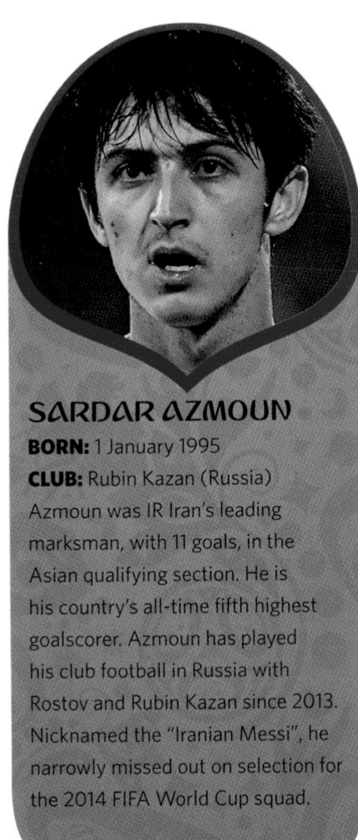

SARDAR AZMOUN

BORN: 1 January 1995

CLUB: Rubin Kazan (Russia)

Azmoun was IR Iran's leading marksman, with 11 goals, in the Asian qualifying section. He is his country's all-time fifth highest goalscorer. Azmoun has played his club football in Russia with Rostov and Rubin Kazan since 2013. Nicknamed the "Iranian Messi", he narrowly missed out on selection for the 2014 FIFA World Cup squad.

RECORD AT PREVIOUS TOURNAMENTS

1930	did not enter
1934	did not enter
1938	did not enter
1950	did not enter
1954	did not enter
1958	did not enter
1962	did not enter
1966	did not enter
1970	did not enter
1974	did not qualify
1978	1st round
1982	withdrew
1986	disqualified
1990	did not qualify
1994	did not qualify
1998	1st round
2002	did not qualify
2006	1st round
2010	did not qualify
2014	1st round

from Azmoun, then drew 0-0 in Seoul. By the time they wrapped up their campaign with a 2-2 home draw against Syria, they were certain of topping the table and heading to Russia.

Such progress was appropriate for a country that had emerged as a major Asian football power back in the 1960s. They won a hat-trick of Asian Championships, collected football gold at the 1974 Asian Games and qualified for the first time for the FIFA World Cup finals in Argentina in 1978. In South America, they marked their finals debut by holding Scotland to a 1-1 draw.

Their progress in the FIFA World Cup was becalmed after the 1979 revolution before they rejoined the finals in 1998 by defeating Australia on away goals in an intercontinental play-off. In France, they achieved their first finals victory by defeating the United States 2-1 in Lyon with goals from Hamid Estili and Mehdi Mahdavikia. A 2-0 defeat by Germany ended their campaign at the first-round group stage.

IR Iran returned to the finals in 2006 but failed again to progress beyond the first round, a tale that would be repeated in Brazil in 2014.

They opened promisingly with a goalless draw against Nigeria, then faced two-time world champions Argentina in Belo Horizonte. For the regulation 90 minutes, their disciplined defending and the goalkeeping of Alireza Haghighi held the Argentinians at bay before Lionel Messi produced a solo special for the decisive goal in the first minute of stoppage time.

Memories of that campaign and the experience gained can only benefit IR Iran in Russia. The squad that brought them through the qualifying competition undefeated includes no fewer several of the 2014 "veterans". These include keeper Haghighi, defender Jalal Hosseini – with more than a century of caps to his name – midfielder Ehsan Hajsafi, captain Dejagah plus forwards Karim Ansarifard and Reza Ghoochannejhad.

Fans will hope that the addition to the squad of free-scoring Sardar Azmoun could make all the difference as they seek to progress beyond the group stage for the first time in Iranian football history.

GROUP C

FRANCE

France bring to the FIFA World Cup™ finals not only the all-round talents of a battle-hardened squad of players but the pride of a nation that boasts historic connection to football's most prestigious tournament.

COACH

DIDIER DESCHAMPS

Deschamps, 49, knows all about the pressures of a FIFA World Cup from his career not only as a coach but as a winning captain. The former Marseille, Juventus and Chelsea midfielder captained France to victory as hosts in 1998 and to UEFA European Championship success two years later. Retirement led to coaching appointments with Monaco, Juventus and Marseille before he took over *Les Bleus* in 2012. Deschamps guided them to the quarter-finals of the FIFA World Cup in Brazil and then to the runners-up slot, as hosts, at UEFA EURO 2016.

Frenchman Jules Rimet was the long-time FIFA President who oversaw the creation of the FIFA World Cup and ensured that France were one of the four European nations who contested the first finals. Not only that, but Lucien Laurent scored, in Uruguay in 1930, the first goal in FIFA World Cup history.

France were only the second European nation to play hosts, in 1938, and in Sweden, 20 years later, centre-forward Just Fontaine set a record that still stands of 13 goals in one tournament. His goals, the majority created by legendary partner Raymond Kopa, led France to third place.

A team led by Michel Platini finished third again in 1986 before their successors, inspired by coach Aimé Jacquet and captain Didier Deschamps, provided France with their first FIFA World Cup success in 1998. The hosts defeated Brazil 3-0 in the final at the Stade de France with two goals from Zinédine Zidane and one from Emmanuel Petit. Two years later, they added the European crown to their world title.

France reached the FIFA World Cup final again in Germany in 2006.

STRIKING OUT FOR THE FINALS: French superstar Antoine Griezmann is the centre of attention at the Stade de France in Saint-Denis after scoring, against Belarus, one of his four goals in European Group A of the qualifying competition.

ONES TO WATCH

ANTOINE GRIEZMANN

BORN: 21 March 1991

CLUB: Atlético Madrid (Spain)

Griezmann, one of European football's most lethal strikers, has played all his club football in Spain with Real Sociedad and now Atlético Madrid. He made his senior France debut in spring 2014, earning selection for the FIFA World Cup later that year. Griezmann was six-goal leading scorer and player of the tournament when the hosts finished runners-up at UEFA EURO 2016.

HUGO LLORIS

BORN: 26 December 1986

CLUB: Tottenham Hotspur (England)

Lloris, captain of France for the past eight years, is one of the most admired goalkeepers in the world game. Born and raised in Nice, he was a European Under-21 champion 2005 and made the first of almost 100 senior appearances three years later. A veteran of the 2010 and 2014 FIFA World Cups, Lloris cost Tottenham €10m when they signed him from Lyon in 2012.

RECORD AT PREVIOUS TOURNAMENTS

1930	1st round
1934	1st round
1938	Quarter-finals
1950	withdrew
1954	1st round
1958	3rd place
1962	did not qualify
1966	1st round
1970	did not qualify
1974	did not qualify
1978	1st round
1982	4th place
1986	3rd place
1990	did not qualify
1994	did not qualify
1998	CHAMPIONS
2002	1st round
2006	Runners-up
2010	1st round
2014	Quarter-finals

They took an early lead through a Zidane penalty before being held 1-1 by Italy and losing a penalty shoot-out.

Coach Raymond Domenech departed in 2010, to be succeeded for a major rebuilding challenge by Laurent Blanc and then Deschamps.

The latter guided France to the quarter-finals in Brazil and then to the runners-up place as hosts at the UEFA European Championship two years ago. The resurgent nucleus of that team then topped the table in European qualifying Group A to secure their ticket to Russia.

The group appeared a challenging one for *Les Bleus*, including as it did the Netherlands, Sweden and Bulgaria plus Luxembourg and Belarus, who held France to a goalless draw in the opening match. Within just over two more months, however, the team were back on track after a 4-1 win over Bulgaria and then a 1-0 win in the Netherlands thanks to a first-half goal from Paul Pogba, who struck again in a 2-1 home win over Sweden.

The only defeat suffered by *Les Bleus* was the visit to Sweden, whom they led by only one point approaching the last matchday. France seized the victory they needed over Belarus in Saint-Denis after first-half goals from Antoine Griezmann and Olivier Giroud. Simultaneously, Sweden lost 2-0 in the Netherlands. France thus ended the campaign four points clear of the Swedes, who entered the play-offs.

Attacking partners Griezmann and Giroud were France's joint leading marksmen, with four goals each in the qualifying competition, followed by two apiece for Pogba, Kévin Gameiro, Thomas Lemar and Dimitri Payet. There was one goal each for Blaise Matuidi and Kylian Mbappé, the brilliant teenager for whom Paris Saint-Germain had agreed to pay Monaco €180m.

In Russia, France must cope with the weight of recent as well as past football history. Old heroes such as Laurent, Fontaine, Kopa and Platini set high standards subsequently emulated by the likes of Zidane, Lilian Thuram, Marcel Desailly, Patrick Vieira – and marksman Thierry Henry with a record 51 goals.

Deschamps himself provides the perfect connection.

GROUP C

AUSTRALIA

Australia always seem to rack up the most air miles in qualifying for the FIFA World Cup™ and this time was no exception. They had to overcome Honduras in the intercontinental play-offs on the road to Russia.

COACH

BERT VAN MARWIJK

Van Marwijk, 65, was appointed in January to succeed Australian Ange Postecoglou, who stepped down after successfully managing the *Socceroos'* qualifying campaign. As a player, he appeared once for the Netherlands, while his club career took him to Go-Ahead Eagles, AZ Alkmaar and MVV Maastricht. After retiring Van Marwijk guided Feyenoord to victory in the 2002 UEFA Cup and also worked in Germany and Saudi Arabia. The high point of his career was in leading the Netherlands to runners-up spot in the 2010 FIFA World Cup South Africa.

The *Socceroos* underwent a minor revolution after Ange Postecoglou took over in 2013. They lost all three of their games at the FIFA World Cup finals in Brazil the following year but progressed to win the AFC Asian Cup on home soil in 2015.

That set them up perfectly for the challenge of qualifying for Russia through the testing Asian system. Australia were seeded directly to the second round, in which they topped Group B ahead of Jordan, Kyrgyzstan, Tajikistan and Bangladesh. They won seven matches and lost only once, 2-0 away to eventual runners-up Jordan in Amman, scoring 29 goals and conceding a mere four.

Captain Mile Jedinak scored their opening goal in a 2-1 victory in Kyrgyzstan while veteran Tim Cahill was their leading marksman with eight goals. His tally included two in the concluding 5-1 win over Jordan, which confirmed Australia in top spot.

The third round was nothing like as straightforward in a difficult Group B. Of the five teams, only Thailand were novices; Japan, Saudi Arabia, United Arab Emirates and Iraq were all previous finalists. On the last

IN SAFE SOCCEROO KEEPING: Goalkeeper Mathew Ryan clears his lines in the second leg of Australia's intercontinental play-off victory over Honduras in Sydney last November. Australia won 3-1 to clinch a place in the finals.

ONES TO WATCH

JOHN "MILE" JEDINAK

BORN: 3 August 1984
CLUB: Aston Villa (England)

Jedinak earned headlines around the world with the hat-trick with which Australia defeated Honduras in the play-offs to reach Russia. The Sydney-born midfielder has played more than 70 times for the *Socceroos* since 2008. He played at both the last two FIFA World Cups and captained Australia to Asian Cup success in 2015.

AARON MOOY

BORN: 15 September 1990
CLUB: Huddersfield Town (England)

Mooy graduated to the *Socceroos* in 2012, three years after appearing at the FIFA U-20 World Cup. He marked his debut with a goal from a free kick against Guam. Mooy launched his career in England with Bolton Wanderers, then returned to Huddersfield Town in 2016 after spells with St Mirren, Melbourne City and Manchester City.

RECORD AT PREVIOUS TOURNAMENTS

1930	did not enter
1934	did not enter
1938	did not enter
1950	did not enter
1954	did not enter
1958	did not enter
1962	did not enter
1966	did not qualify
1970	did not qualify
1974	1st round
1978	did not qualify
1982	did not qualify
1986	did not qualify
1990	did not qualify
1994	did not qualify
1998	did not qualify
2002	did not qualify
2006	Round of 16
2010	1st round
2014	1st round

matchday, Australia needed to win at home to Thailand to clinch their passage to Russia and hope that Saudi Arabia did not beat the already qualified Japan in Jeddah.

Goals from Tomi Juric and Matthew Leckie brought a 2-1 win over Thailand, but the Saudis defeated Japan 1-0 to claim second place on goal difference. Third-placed Australia thus entered the Asian play-offs, where they needed extra time in Sydney to overcome Syria 2-1 and thus 3-2 on aggregate. Cahill scored both goals to earn an intercontinental play-off against Honduras from CONCACAF.

Solid defending earned a goalless draw away in San Pedro Sula before a hat-trick from skipper Jedinak, including two penalties, earned a 3-1 victory back at Stadium Australia. After 22 games all around Asia and across the world, Australia had made it to the finals for the fourth time in succession and fifth in all.

This team bears only a passing resemblance to the outfit on view in Brazil in 2014. The squad has been drawn from as far afield as England, Scotland, Austria, Belgium, Germany, the Netherlands, Switzerland, Turkey, Israel, Japan and Saudi Arabia.

The "English contingent" included goalkeeper Matt Ryan (Brighton & Hove Albion), goalscoring captain Jedinak (Aston Villa), midfielders Aaron Mooy (Huddersfield Town) and Massimo Luongo (Queens Park Rangers), and 38-year-old striker Cahill (who rejoined Millwall) while firepower in attack was generated by German-based Leckie (Hertha BSC) and Robbie Kruse (VfL Bochum). Bert van Marwyk took over as coach after Postezoglu left following qualification.

Australia's FIFA World Cup consistency has helped raise football's profile in a sports-crazy country amid competition from Aussie Rules, both codes of rugby and cricket.

Football Federation Australia was founded only in 1963 (it was then called the Australian Soccer Federation) and their FIFA World Cup debut followed 13 years later in West Germany. Their best showing, in reaching the round of 16, was in 2006 immediately before Australia transferred from the Oceania Football Confederation to its Asian football "neighbour".

GROUP C

PERU

No nation with previous FIFA World Cup™ experience has been absent from the finals as long as Peru. Their last appearance was in 1982, so it was no wonder the government marked qualification with a national holiday.

COACH

RICARDO GARECA

Gareca, 60, is a former Argentina international centre-forward who took over Peru in 2015. Within weeks he had guided them to the semi-finals of the *Copa América*. This was "el Tigre's" first national team job after club appointments in Argentina, Colombia, Peru and Brazil. As a centre-forward, Gareca scored, against Peru, the goal that qualified Argentina for the finals of the 1986 FIFA World Cup. However, he was omitted from the1 squad that would go on to win in Mexico. Gareca played for both Buenos Aires giants River Plate and Boca Juniors and won league titles with Independiente in Argentina and América de Cali in Colombia.

Public sector workers were given the day off and schools were closed after goals from Jefferson Farfán and Christian Ramos provided a 2-0 victory over New Zealand in the second leg of the intercontinental play-off.

"Thank you, warriors, for giving us such joy," said state President Pablo Kuczynski in a tweeted message of congratulations to the players and their Argentinian coach, Ricardo Gareca. Fans thronged the squares and streets of Lima and other cities in celebration.

Lima and its clubs have dominated football in Peru ever since the football association was founded there in 1922. The local Lima league was always the strongest in the country and the top title-winners are Lima clubs Universitario (26), Alianza (22) and Sporting Cristal (18).

Peru's international debut came in the South American Championship of 1927 and they won the event on home soil in 1939. They have won the *Copa América* on only one other occasion, in 1975, during the national team's so-called "golden era" when they also qualified three

ENDING A VERY LONG WAIT: Christian Ramos celebrates after scoring Peru's second goal in the 2-0 defeat of New Zealand in Lima, in the second leg of the qualifying play-off which lifted the hosts into the finals of the FIFA World Cup for the first time in 36 years.

ONES TO WATCH

JEFFERSON FARFÁN

BORN: 26 October 1984

CLUB: Lokomotiv Moscow (Russia)

Farfán knows all about playing conditions in Russia, having been playing there since January 2017 with Lokomotiv Moscow. Until now, the forward's FIFA World Cup experience had been limited to the qualifying competitions for 2006, 2010 and 2014. He overcame serious knee trouble to return to duty for the *Copa América* in 2015.

EDISON FLORES

BORN: 14 May 1994

CLUBS: Universitario (Per), Villareal B (Esp), Aalborg (Den)

Flores was Peru's five-goal leading marksman from midfield in the South American qualifiers. He was discovered by his hero Héctor Chumpitaz and was already playing for Universitario when he starred at the U-17 Copa Libertadores in 2011. Later he moved to Villareal in Spain before joining Aalborg in 2016.

RECORD AT PREVIOUS TOURNAMENTS

1930	1st round
1934	withdrew
1938	did not enter
1950	withdrew
1954	withdrew
1958	did not qualify
1962	did not qualify
1966	did not qualify
1970	Quarter-finals
1974	did not qualify
1978	2nd round
1982	1st round
1986	did not qualify
1990	did not qualify
1994	did not qualify
1998	did not qualify
2002	did not qualify
2006	did not qualify
2010	did not qualify
2014	did not qualify

times for the FIFA World Cup.

The first time Peru appeared in the finals of the FIFA World Cup helped to create history at the inaugural tournament in Uruguay in 1930. However, Peru failed to progress beyond the opening round, and did not appear on the grand stage for another 40 years. In Mexico in 1970 a fine side starring all-time Peruvian greats such as Teófilo Cubillas, Hugo Sotil and Héctor Chumpitaz achieved their finest finish by reaching the quarter-finals.

Chumpitaz, Sotil and Cubillas were still on hand when Peru reached the second round mini-league in Argentina in 1978. But only Cubillas was still there when Peru faded out in the first round in Spain in 1982.

The latest generation of fan favourites first made their reviving presence felt at the *Copa América* in 2015, when they reached the semi-finals, and they maintained their momentum in the World Cup qualifying competition.

In goal was Pedro Gallese from Mexico's Veracruz behind a defence marshalled by veteran captain Alberto Rodríguez from Universitario and supported by Christian Ramos and Luis Advíncula who, after more than 60 caps, ended the qualifiers still looking for his first goal in seven years of international football.

Similar levels of experience were provided in midfield by Yoshimar Yotún and Christian Cueva from Orlando City and Sao Paulo FC respectively. For its goals, the team depends, as it has done for more than a decade, on Paolo Guerrero and Farfán, who has lately been playing his club football in Russia with Lokomotiv Moscow.

Guerrero and Edison Flores were Peru's leading marksmen in the South American qualifying competition, with five goals. Peru were a modest 50th in the FIFA/Coca-Cola World Ranking when they began with defeats away to Colombia and at home to Chile. Eventually they secured fifth place in the table and a play-off chance with a 1-1 home draw against Colombia in the last round of matches.

Victory over New Zealand – 0-0 away, 2-0 at home – thus opened the door to Russia and ended a very long wait.

GROUP C

DENMARK

Resurgent Denmark approach the FIFA World Cup™ intent on making up for lost time after missing out on Brazil in 2014. Coach Åge Hareide is seeking to rekindle the famed "Danish Dynamite" around Christian Eriksen.

COACH

ÅGE HAREIDE

Hareide, 64, succeeded Morten Olsen in 2016 after becoming the only coach to win league titles with clubs in three Nordic countries: Rosenborg in Norway, Helsingborgs in Sweden and Brøndby IF in Denmark. Hareide also coached Örgryte and Malmo in Sweden after five years as boss of Norway between 2003 and 2008. Earlier, Hareide had launched his playing career with Hødd and then Molde IK. He spent almost a decade in English football, playing in attack and midfield for Manchester City and Norwich City before ending his career back at Molde.

The Danes emerged from the qualifying campaign via the play-offs with a squad benefiting from the experience offered by defender Simon Kjær, and midfielders Eriksen and William Kvist, all veterans of the campaign in South Africa.

Kasper Schmeichel has established himself in goal. The son of Peter Schmeichel provides a link back to the high point of Danish football, when they reached the round of 16 at the 1986 FIFA World Cup in Mexico and then proceeded to win the 1992 UEFA European Football Championship in neighbouring Sweden.

Other senior members of the latest generation include defenders Andreas Bjelland and Peter Ankersen, midfielders Lasse Schöne and Thomas Delaney as well as forwards Nicolai Jørgensen and Yussuf Poulsen.

Denmark was one of the first countries in continental Europe to take up football and has some of the oldest clubs in the world. In the years before the FIFA World Cup was established, they enjoyed early success at the Summer Olympics. They were the winners

EXPLODING BACK AMONG THE ELITE: Christian Eriksen (left) celebrates with team-mates Nicklas Bendtner (11) and Thomas Delaney (8) after shooting Denmark ahead from a penalty in their 1-1 qualifying draw against Romania in Copenhagen.

ONES TO WATCH

KASPER SCHMEICHEL

BORN: 5 November 1986

CLUB: Leicester City (England)

Schmeichel has followed his father, Peter, in establishing himself as a key member of Denmark's squad. He played regularly for the U-21s and has won more than 30 caps since his debut in 2013. Schmeichel's talent and experience were a major contribution to Leicester City's surprise English Premier League title success in 2016

NICKLAS BENDTNER

BORN: 16 January 1988

CLUB: Rosenborg (Norway)

Bendtner, with 30 goals from 80 caps, was launched as a teenager by Arsenal. He played at all youth levels for Denmark and marked his senior debut at 18 with a goal against Poland in 2006. He played for Denmark at the 2010 FIFA World Cup while his club career took him to Italy's Juventus, among other clubs, before he joined Rosenborg last year.

RECORD AT PREVIOUS TOURNAMENTS

1930	did not enter
1934	did not enter
1938	did not enter
1950	did not enter
1954	did not enter
1958	did not qualify
1962	did not enter
1966	did not qualify
1970	did not qualify
1974	did not qualify
1978	did not qualify
1982	did not qualify
1986	Round of 16
1990	did not qualify
1994	did not qualify
1998	Quarter-finals
2002	Round of 16
2006	did not qualify
2010	1st round
2014	did not qualify

in 1906 and runners-up in 1908 and 1912, their outstanding players including Nils Middelboe, who later played for Chelsea.

A subsequent period of decline ended after a reorganisation of the domestic game was rewarded in the 1970s. Stars such as 1977 European Footballer of the Year Allan Simonsen were lured abroad but brought their new-found experience back to the benefit of the national team.

Players such as Simonsen, Preben Elkjær, Morten Olsen and the Laudrup brothers Brian and Michael formed the nucleus of the "Danish Dynamite" side of the 1980s and early 1990s. Denmark were also impressive at the 1998 FIFA World Cup in France, reaching the quarter-finals before falling to Brazil. They reached the round of 16 in 2002 but missed out in 2006, flew home after the first round in 2010 and did not qualify again in 2014.

The campaign to make amends in Russia was undertaken in European Group E. Denmark lost only twice in their ten games, 3-2 away to Poland and then three days later 1-0 at home to Montenegro. However, those defeats made it impossible for Hareide's men to make up lost ground on the Poles, who finished five points clear at the top of the table.

Denmark secured the runners-up spot and a play-offs place by finishing five points clear of the Montenegrins. With eight goals conceded, they had the best defensive record in the group while Eriksen (eight goals) and Delaney (four) were their leading marksmen.

The play-offs draw matched Denmark with the Republic of Ireland. They were held to a goalless draw in Copenhagen, but then struck a rich vein of form to win 5-1 in Dublin.

The Irish were dreaming briefly of Russia when Shane Duffy headed them into an early lead, but Denmark soon levelled through an own goal. After that it was the Eriksen show: the Tottenham playmaker scored a superb hat-trick before Nicklas Bendtner rounded off the scoring with a late penalty. Denmark were back in the finals - and back in style, prompting comparisons with the team who starred at the finals three decades ago.

GROUP D

ARGENTINA

Argentina are one of the great football powers, twice champions of the world and runners-up on three occasions. The country has produced some of the game's finest players including current superstar Lionel Messi.

COACH

JORGE SAMPAOLI

Sampaoli, 58, turned Argentina's fortunes around after a stuttering start to their qualifying campaign. He was appointed to succeed Edgardo Bauza last June after one season in charge of Spanish club Sevilla. He already had FIFA World Cup experience, having led Chile to the round of 16 at the finals in Brazil in 2014. The following year he led Chile to their first-ever success in the *Copa América* – against Argentina. Sampaoli's club career has included spells not only in Chile and Spain but also in Argentina, Peru and Ecuador.

The roll of honour for the *Albiceleste* also includes 14 victories in the *Copa América*, Olympic gold medals on two occasions plus a further triumph in the 1992 FIFA Confederations Cup.

Argentina's football history is not only a proud one but a long one. The British brought football to the country in the 1860s and the Argentine Football Association was founded in 1893 by an English schoolteacher, Alexander Hutton. A league was set up the same year, and in 1901 the national side met Uruguay in the first international match to be staged outside Great Britain.

Professionalism was adopted in the early 1930s, when the Buenos Aires giants River Plate and Boca Juniors emerged as dominant forces of the domestic club game.

Argentina were runners-up to Uruguay in the 1928 Summer Olympics, then lost 4-2 to their neighbours in the 1930 FIFA World Cup Final (the first ever). Great players headed by the likes of Alfredo di Stéfano and Omar Sívori were attracted to clubs in Spain and Italy over the ensuing decades.

HEADING BACK TO THE FINALS: Captain Lionel Messi (10) and his Argentina team-mates make the most of the moment after the country's 3-1 win away to Ecuador in Quito last October secured third place in the South America qualifying group and a ticket to Russia.

ONES TO WATCH

ÁNGEL DI MARÍA

BORN: 14 February 1988
CLUB: Paris Saint-Germain (France)

Di María was a key member of the Argentina team that finished runners-up at the 2104 FIFA World Cup. A versatile, wide-ranging winger, he also scored Argentina's Olympic gold medal-winning goal against Nigeria in 2008. His club career has taken him to Rosario Central, Benfica, Real Madrid and Manchester United as well as PSG.

JAVIER MASCHERANO

BORN: 8 June 1984
CLUB: FC Barcelona (Spain)

Mascherano has been a stalwart of the national team, in midfield or central defence, for 15 years and on more than 140 occasions during a successful club career with River Plate, Brazil's Corinthians, Liverpool in England and FC Barcelona. He was a South American U-20 champion and was a member of Argentina's gold medal team at the 2008 Summer Olympic Games in Beijing.

RECORD AT PREVIOUS TOURNAMENTS

1930	Runners-up
1934	1st round
1938	did not enter
1950	did not enter
1954	did not enter
1958	1st round
1962	1st round
1966	Quarter-finals
1970	did not qualify
1974	2nd round
1978	CHAMPIONS
1982	2nd round
1986	CHAMPIONS
1990	Runners-up
1994	Round of 16
1998	Quarter-finals
2002	1st round
2006	Quarter-finals
2010	Quarter-finals
2014	Runners-up

Argentina returned to the FIFA World Cup finals in 1958, 1962 and 1966 while the country's club teams recorded a series of successes in their own South American international competitions.

FIFA World Cup success eluded Argentina until 1978 when, as hosts, they defeated the Netherlands 3-1 in the Final in Buenos Aires. Striker Mario Kempes was the top scorer with six goals, including two in the Final. They enjoyed FIFA World Cup glory again eight years later, when captain Diego Maradona inspired them to victory in Mexico in 1986.

Argentina were runners-up in 1990 and then again in Brazil four years ago when Lionel Messi won the Golden Ball as player of the tournament. They were also runners-up to Chile in both the *Copa América* in 2015 and the *Copa America Centenario* in the United States in 2016.

In the qualifying campaign, Messi and his team-mates enjoyed a winning start by defeating Uruguay 1-0, but then drew with Venezuela and Peru before losing to Paraguay and Brazil.

A new manager, Jorge Sampaoli, was appointed last June. He got off to a flying start in two friendlies, Argentina scoring a 1-0 success against Brazil in Melbourne and then a 6-0 victory over Singapore. But the last stages of the FIFA World Cup qualifying campaign proved much more awkward.

Argentina were held to draws by Uruguay, Venezuela and Peru and thus reached the last round of matches sitting outside the four guaranteed qualifying places. Their prospects of a place in the finals in Russia hung in the balance.

The concluding match, which they had to win, was away to Ecuador, who took the lead in the first minute. Argentina recovered, however, to win 3-1 with a hat-trick from Messi. He finished as Argentina's leading scorer, with seven goals, in the South American qualifying section.

Other experienced squad members included goalkeeper Sergio Romero, central defenders Javier Mascherano and Nicolás Otamendi, midfielders Lucas Biglia and Éver Banega plus forwards Ángel di María and Paulo Dybala.

GROUP D

ICELAND

Iceland are appearing at the FIFA World Cup™ finals for the first time in Russia, but no one will dare underrate them after their headline-grabbing progress to the quarter-finals of the 2016 UEFA European Championship.

COACH

HEIMIR HALLGRÍMSSON

Hallgrímsson, 50, built on the work accomplished with predecessor Lars Lagerbäck during the 2016 UEFA European Championship. He took over as sole national coach before the FIFA World Cup qualifying campaign. Previously Hallgrímsson, a dentist, spent most of his playing career with IBV Vestmannaeyjar before turning to coaching. He had separate spells managing the IBV men and women's teams before joining the Icelandic FA coaching staff as assistant to Lagerbäck in October 2011. Before the UEFA EURO campaign, the two were appointed as joint managers.

Their fans' "Viking war chant" caught the imagination of supporters around the world. Any suspicions that Iceland's performance in France was a brief encounter were quashed by their FIFA World Cup qualifying success, some 124 years since football "arrived" in the country.

James Ferguson, a Scottish printer and bookseller, was the pioneer whose enthusiasm led to the creation of an Athletic Union and championship in 1912. The first winners were KR Reykjavik, who have the most league titles to their name with 26. In 1964 KR also became the first Icelandic club to test the competitive waters in Europe.

By that time, a national team had long been in existence. Iceland made their international debut on 17 July 1946, with a 3-0 home defeat by Denmark, from whom Iceland had secured independence only two years earlier. Iceland's first victory came in 1947 with a 2-0 win over Finland in Reykjavik.

Their first FIFA World Cup qualifying attempt was for the 1958 tournament with a team including their original star forward in Albert Guðmundsson, who later played for

ACHIEVING THE BREAKTHROUGH: Johann Berg Gudmundsson (left) and forward Alfred Finnbogason (11) share the joy of history after Iceland reach the FIFA World Cup finals for the first time with their 2-0 defeat of Kosovo in Reykjavik.

ONES TO WATCH

GYLFI SIGURÐSSON

BORN: 8 September 1989

CLUB: Everton (England)

Sigurðsson is one of the most effective creative midfielders in the English Premier League. He has never played senior football in Iceland, having moved to England as a youth player with Reading in 2005. Later he played in Germany for TSG Hoffenheim before returning to British football with Swansea City (twice), Tottenham Hotspur and now Everton, whom he joined last summer.

ARON GUNNARSSON

BORN: 22 April 1989

CLUB: Cardiff City (Wales)

Gunnarsson is one of Iceland's most experienced players, with more than 70 caps since his debut in 2008. A right-back or central midfielder, he began with Thór Akureyri but has played most of his career in the UK with Coventry City and then Cardiff City, with whom he was a League Cup runner-up in 2012. Gunnarson has been Iceland's captain since taking over the armband in mid-2012.

RECORD AT PREVIOUS TOURNAMENTS

1930	did not enter
1934	did not enter
1938	did not enter
1950	did not enter
1954	entry application rejected
1958	did not qualify
1962	did not enter
1966	did not enter
1970	did not enter
1974	did not qualify
1978	did not qualify
1982	did not qualify
1986	did not qualify
1990	did not qualify
1994	did not qualify
1998	did not qualify
2002	did not qualify
2006	did not qualify
2010	did not qualify
2014	did not qualify

Arsenal, AC Milan and AS Nancy-Lorraine.

Other Icelandic footballers to make their mark abroad have included defender and later national coach Atli Eðvaldsson at Celtic, striker Pétur Pétursson at Feyenoord, and midfield general Ásgeir Sigurvinsson in Belgium with Standard Liège and then in Germany with Stuttgart. Eiður Guðjohnsen, the country's top scorer with a record 26 goals, further underlined Iceland's potential, by finding success at Chelsea and Barcelona.

Such was the progress within the domestic game that Iceland had been managed by home-grown coaches for two decades until Sweden's Lars Lagerbäck joined Heimir Hallgrímsson for the UEFA EURO 2016 campaign. Hallgrímsson then took up sole charge for the FIFA World Cup qualifying campaign.

Croatia, Ukraine and Turkey provided opposition with finals pedigree, but Iceland were buoyed by their achievement in France as well as memories of the 2014 FIFA World Cup campaign, when they were denied a place in the finals in Brazil only after a play-off against Croatia.

Iceland opened by gaining a 1-1 draw in Ukraine. Alfreð Finnbogason, leading marksman in the Dutch league in 2013-14, struck the opening goal after six minutes. He was on target in the subsequent 3-2 home win over Finland when Iceland, in front of their own fans, turned the match on its head with two goals in second-half stoppage time.

Finnbogason struck for a third successive time in a 2-0 home win over Turkey before Iceland suffered their first defeat, 2-0 in Croatia. They lost only one more game, by 1-0 in Finland last September. Hence Hallgrímsson's men went into their concluding tie, at home to Kosovo, knowing that victory would ensure historic qualification.

Gylfi Sigurðsson and Jóhann Guðmundsson struck either side of half-time to seal Iceland's place in Russia and also make history as the smallest nation (population 335,000) to do so. Hallgrímsson was almost lost for words, saying: "This is really odd, I don't know what to say. I mean: Pelé, Maradona ... and Aron Einar Gunnarsson."

GROUP D

CROATIA

Croatia finished third on their FIFA World Cup™ finals debut in 1998 and have never come close to matching that achievement. Their eagerness to rekindle their old glory was evident in their decisive progress through the play-offs.

COACH

ZLATKO DALIĆ

Dalić, 51, succeeded Ante Čačić as manager of Croatia after their penultimate qualifying tie against Finland had ended in a 1-1 draw. Previously Dalić had led the U-21s between 2006 and 2011. At club level, he coached Varteks, Rijeka, Slaven Belupo and Albania's Dinamo Tirana before heading for the Middle East, where he coached Al-Faisaly and Al-Hilal in Saudi Arabia, then Al-Ain in the United Arab Emirates. That team won the Arabian Gulf League and the UAE Super Cup in 2015 and were then runners-up in the AFC Champions League 2016.

Greece stood in the Croats' way at the end of the European qualifying process. But not for long. The first leg, on home soil in Zagreb, saw Croatia rush into a two-goal lead inside the first 20 minutes courtesy of goals from playmaker Luka Modrić (penalty) and Nikola Kalinić. Croatia celebrated a 4-1 success at the final whistle and went on to hold out for a goalless draw in Piraeus.

The squad heading for Russia includes a wealth of international experience at both country and club levels. In midfield, captain Modrić from Real Madrid and Barcelona's Ivan Rakitić have set aside their Spanish *Clásico* rivalry in the national cause, supported by Ivan Perišić and Marcelo Brozović, from Italy's Internazionale, who create the openings for two more Italian *Serie A* stalwarts in Juventus's Mario Mandžukić and Milan's Kalinić.

In defence, resistance to whatever the opposition may offer has been led by Domagoj Vida from Dynamo Kiev, Sampdoria's Ivan Strinić and Liverpool's Dejan Lovren playing in front of goalkeeper Danijel Subašić from French Champions League regulars Monaco, French regulars

WINNING AGAINST THE ODDS: Andrej Kramarić (kneeling) and his team-mates enjoy achieving a breakthrough after he scores the first of his two goals in Croatia's crucial 2-0 victory away to Ukraine at the Olympic Stadium in Kiev.

ONES TO WATCH

LUKA MODRIĆ

BORN: 9 September 1985

CLUB: Real Madrid (Spain)

Modrić, captain and playmaker of Croatia, knows all about success at international level after winning the FIFA Club World Cup and three UEFA Champions League titles with Real Madrid. He has scored a dozen goals in more than 100 games for Croatia since his debut in 2006. He has also played for Dinamo Zagreb and Tottenham Hotspur.

MARIO MANDŽUKIĆ

BORN: 21 May 1986

CLUB: Juventus (Italy)

Mandžukić has been leading the line with enormous power for both Croatia and Italy's Juventus recently. He has scored 30 goals in 90-plus internationals, including five in the qualifiers. He was also named Croatia's Player of the Year in 2012 and 2013. His career has also taken him to Dinamo Zagreb, VfL Wolfsburg, Bayern Munich and Atlético Madrid.

RECORD AT PREVIOUS TOURNAMENTS

1930	did not exist
1934	did not exist
1938	did not exist
1950	did not exist
1954	did not exist
1958	did not exist
1962	did not exist
1966	did not exist
1970	did not exist
1974	did not exist
1978	did not exist
1982	did not exist
1986	did not exist
1990	did not exist
1994	unable to enter
1998	3rd place
2002	1st round
2006	1st round
2010	did not qualify
2014	1st round

in recent seasons in the UEFA Champions League.

Remarkably, for a nation that boasts a consistently high profile in the international arena, Croatia emerged as an independent nation only at the start of the 1990s after the fragmentation of Yugoslavia.

They quickly made an impact. They reached the quarter-finals of the UEFA European Championship in 1996, beating Italy on the way, and then stormed to third place in France at the 1998 FIFA World Cup. Key players included Zvonimir Boban, Davor Šuker and Robert Prosinečki (all FIFA World Youth champions with the former Yugoslavia in 1987). Šuker, who is now the president of the Croatian FA, scored six goals in France to win the Golden Boot as the tournament's leading scorer.

Since then, Croatia have been regular contenders in both FIFA World Cups and UEFA European Championships, missing out only once on each finals tournament. Third place remains their best finish at the FIFA World Cup while they reached the UEFA EURO quarter-finals twice and progressed to the round of 16 in France in 2016.

Two months later, Croatia launched their FIFA World Cup qualifying campaign in Group I of the European section with a 1-1 draw at home to Turkey. Midfielder Rakitić opened their account from a penalty shortly before half-time. They followed that up by seizing early command of the group with victories over Kosovo, Finland, Iceland and Ukraine. Defeats away to Iceland and Turkey and a home draw against Finland, however, threw their hopes into doubt.

The Croatian FA decided that a new approach was needed ahead of the decisive last game in Ukraine and replaced coach Ante Čačić with Zlatko Dalić. The prize at stake for both teams was second place behind Iceland, but it was Croatia who took the play-off spot by winning 2-0 in Kiev with a second-half double from Andrej Kramarić.

Victory over Greece in the play-offs then duly set Modrić, Mandžukić and their team-mates on the road to the finals for the fifth time in six FIFA World Cups. Within weeks Modrić earned more international kudos after helping lead Real Madrid to FIFA Club World Cup success.

GROUP D

NIGERIA

Nigeria, three times African champions, have now reached the FIFA World Cup™ finals six times in seven editions and, under veteran coach Gernot Rohr, want to go beyond the round of 16 for the first time in their proud history.

COACH

GERNOT ROHR

Rohr, 64, was born in Mannheim, Germany, and has been a French citizen since 1982. He played in defence and midfield for Bayern Munich and Waldhof Mannheim before winning the French league title three times in the 1980s with Bordeaux. He played five times for West Germany at amateur level. Rohr worked as a club coach in France, Germany, Austria, Switzerland and Tunisia before 2010, when he began specialising in African national teams. He coached Gabon, Niger and Burkina Faso before taking up his current appointment with Nigeria in August 2016.

The *Super Eagles* have the pedigree and the talent, which their youth teams have displayed consistently. The *Golden Eaglets* have won the FIFA U-17 World Cup five times and, in 1996, they became the first African nation to win Olympic gold in what is, predominantly, a U-23 competition.

A football association was founded in 1945 in Nigeria, which is Africa's most populous country (300m). A national team had played unofficial matches against neighbours since the early 1930s, but it did not "take off" until after the country achieved independence in 1960. The NFA had already taken the necessary steps to join FIFA and the Confederation of African Football and entered the FIFA World Cup qualifying competition for the first time in 1961.

Progress was marked by qualification for the final stages of the Africa Cup of Nations in 1963 and then a first main stage appearance in the 1968 Summer Olympics in Mexico City. The next year they lost out to Morocco on the toss of a coin in pursuit of a place in the FIFA World Cup finals. In 1980,

BACK IN THE BIG TIME: In October 2017 Nigeria's Alex Iwobi (centre) was the focus of attention after scoring the only goal of the game against Zambia in front of 80,000 fans in Uyo, ensuring the *Super Eagles* became the first African nation to qualify for the finals in Russia.

ONES TO WATCH

AHMED MUSA

BORN: 14 October 1992

CLUB: Leicester City (England)

Musa made history at the 2014 FIFA World Cup when he became, against Argentina, the first Nigerian player to score more than once in a match in the finals. He began with the GBS Football Academy and played in the Netherlands and Russia before joining Leicester City in 2016. He made his senior international debut for Nigeria's *Super Eagles* in 2010.

VICTOR MOSES

BORN: 12 December 1990

CLUB: Chelsea (England)

Moses was born in Lagos and moved to London at the age of 11. He played for Crystal Palace and Wigan Athletic before joining Chelsea in 2012. After loan spells with various clubs he returned to be a key member, as a raiding wing-back, of the 2016-17 Premier League title winners. Moses played for England at youth level but switched back to Nigeria in 2012.

RECORD AT PREVIOUS TOURNAMENTS

1930	did not enter
1934	did not enter
1938	did not enter
1950	did not enter
1954	did not enter
1958	did not enter
1962	did not qualify
1966	withdrew
1970	did not qualify
1974	did not qualify
1978	did not qualify
1982	did not qualify
1986	did not qualify
1990	did not qualify
1994	Round of 16
1998	Round of 16
2002	1st round
2006	did not qualify
2010	1st round
2014	Round of 16

they won the Africa Cup of Nations for the first time.

Finally, in the 1990s, Nigeria fulfilled their promise on the world stage by twice reaching the round of 16 at the FIFA World Cup – in the United States in 1994 and then again in France in 1998.

In 1994 Nigeria, newly crowned African champions for a second time, nearly sprang one of the greatest of surprises. They topped their first-round group – ahead of Argentina, Bulgaria and Greece – and were eliminated 2-1 by Italy only after extra time. In 1998, a team starring goalkeeper Peter Rufai, midfielder Jay-Jay Okocha and winger Finidi George, beat Spain 3-2 in their opening game, before being knocked out 4-1 by Denmark.

Between 2000 and 2010, Nigeria were regular contenders in the knockout stages of the Africa Cup of Nations. In 2002 and 2010, they lost in the first round at the FIFA World Cup finals and then in 2014, as African champions, reached the round of 16 in Brazil, when a team now led by star goalkeeper Vincent Enyeama, Joseph Yobo, Ahmed Musa, John Obi Mikel and Victor Moses lost 2-0 to France.

Musa was promoted to captain by the time Nigeria launched their qualification bid for Russia 2018 in the African second round in a 2-0 aggregate win over Swaziland. That took them into the third round comprising five groups of four teams, with the winners advancing to the finals.

Nigeria were grouped with Zambia, Cameroon and Algeria. On paper it appeared a difficult group, but the *Super Eagles* took immediate command by winning 2-1 in Zambia, 3-1 at home to Algeria and 4-0 at home to Cameroon. A 1-0 home win over Zambia on 7 October last year saw coach Rohr's men become the first African nation to reach Russia 2018. Arsenal's Alex Iwobi, nephew of three-time FIFA World Cup veteran Jay-Jay Okocha, scored the goal that sent Nigeria to their sixth finals.

Their qualification survived the alteration by FIFA of a 1-1 draw away to Algeria on the last matchday into a 3-0 defeat because Nigeria had fielded suspended and thus ineligible Abdullahi Shehu.

GROUP E

BRAZIL

Brazil go to Russia defending their status as the greatest nation in the history of the FIFA World Cup™. They have triumphed a record five times, finished runners-up twice and are the only ever-present finalists.

COACH

TITE (Adenor Leonardo Bacchi)

Tite, 58, celebrated his first achievement as national coach after only eight months in the job when Brazil secured their place in the finals last year. He had taken over from former FIFA World Cup-winning captain Dunga in June 2016. Tite spent 11 years as a defensive midfielder with home town Caxias do Sol, Esportivo, Portuguesa (São Paulo) and Guarani. He began a 28-year coaching career with Caxias. Most notably, he guided Corinthians to success in the Brazilian championship twice as well as the *Copa Libertadores* and the 2012 FIFA Club World Cup.

Beyond the statistics, Brazil have also brought their *Jogo Bonito* (Beautiful Game) to the FIFA World Cup through the explosive technical brilliance of legendary players such as Pelé, Garrincha, Didi, Romário, Bebeto, Ronaldo and Ronaldinho.

The latest superstar is Neymar, who made his finals debut on home soil in 2014 and cemented his reputation with the penalty that won Olympic gold for Brazil in Rio de Janeiro in 2016.

Brazilian football developed at the end of the nineteenth century, prompted by migrant British workers, with leagues established in Rio and São Paulo by the turn of the century. The national team entered the competitive arena at the South American Championship in 1916. They competed modestly at the 1930 and 1934 FIFA World Cups, then reached the semi-finals in France in 1938 before losing to champions Italy.

A golden age then followed between 1950 and 1970. Brazil, as hosts, were FIFA World Cup runners-up to Uruguay in 1950, reached the quarter-finals in 1954 and then won for the first time in Sweden in 1958. A forward line featuring Garrincha,

PUTTING THE MESSAGE ACROSS: Left to right, Philippe Coutinho, Neymar and Gabriel Jesus tell the world that Brazil are back on track after beating old rivals Argentina 3-0 in Belo Horizonte in a South American qualifying tie in November 2016.

ONES TO WATCH

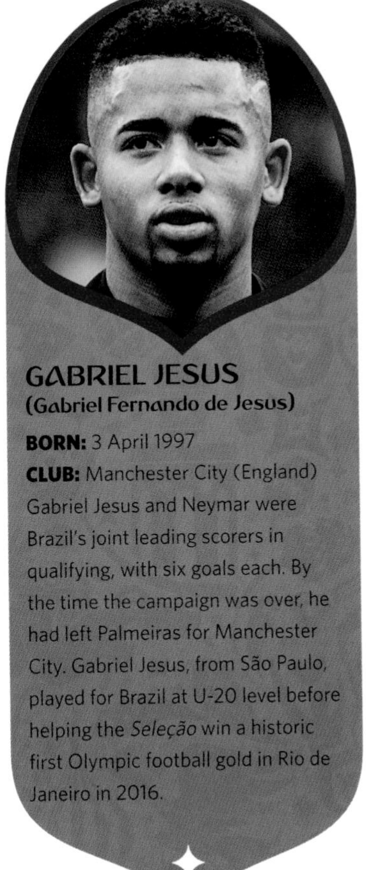

GABRIEL JESUS

(Gabriel Fernando de Jesus)

BORN: 3 April 1997

CLUB: Manchester City (England)

Gabriel Jesus and Neymar were Brazil's joint leading scorers in qualifying, with six goals each. By the time the campaign was over, he had left Palmeiras for Manchester City. Gabriel Jesus, from São Paulo, played for Brazil at U-20 level before helping the *Seleção* win a historic first Olympic football gold in Rio de Janeiro in 2016.

MARCELO

(Marcelo Vieira da Silva Júnior)

BORN: 12 May 1988

CLUB: Real Madrid (Spain)

Marcelo is the latest in a long line of brilliant Brazil left-backs stretching back via Roberto Carlos and Júnior to Nílton Santos. He starred for Fluminense in his home city of Rio de Janeiro before joining Real Madrid in 2007. He has since won 14 major club titles as well as the FIFA Confederations Cup with Brazil in 2013.

RECORD AT PREVIOUS TOURNAMENTS

1930	1st round
1934	1st round
1938	3rd place
1950	Runners-up
1954	Quarter-finals
1958	CHAMPIONS
1962	CHAMPIONS
1966	1st round
1970	CHAMPIONS
1974	4th place
1978	2nd round
1982	2nd round
1986	Quarter-finals
1990	2nd round
1994	CHAMPIONS
1998	Runners-up
2002	CHAMPIONS
2006	Quarter-finals
2010	Quarter-finals
2014	4th place

Vavá, Zagallo and the 17-year-old Pelé strolled to a 5-2 win over their hosts in the final. In Chile, in 1962, an almost identical team, minus the injured Pelé, beat Czechoslovakia 3-1 to defend their title.

Brazil clinched a hat-trick in Mexico in 1970. The brilliance of Pelé, supported by the likes of Tostão, Gérson, Jairzinho and Carlos Alberto, earned Brazil the right to keep the Jules Rimet Trophy forever. Further success was achieved in 1994, against Italy in Pasadena, via the first penalty shoot-out in a final. Title number five, secured with a win over Germany, was inspired by Ronaldo in 2002 at the finals hosted by Japan and Korea Republic.

Brazil are still awaiting their sixth crown. The quarter-finals were the end of the road in 2006 and 2010, and the team ended in fourth place when they played host four years ago. Major changes followed, both on and off the pitch. Luiz Felipe Scolari was succeeded as coach by Dunga and then by Tite after Brazil fell short in both the 2015 *Copa América* and the 2016 *Copa América Centenario*.

Under Dunga, Brazil had made a slow start to qualifying for Russia with a 2-0 defeat in Chile and draws against Argentina, Uruguay and Paraguay in their first six matches. By the time qualifying resumed, in September 2016, Tite had taken over. Brazil duly won all of their next nine qualifying ties to secure their place in Russia with four games remaining.

Gabriel Jesus and Neymar scored six goals apiece with midfielders Willian and Philippe Coutinho contributing four each. Brazil also owe their place in Russia to solid defensive work. Dani Alves, Thiago Silva, Marcelo, Miranda and Marquinhos offer enormous international experience behind hard-working midfield cover from the likes of Paulinho, Fernandinho, Renato Augusto and Casemiro.

The sum total of all of these talents was evident in the outcome of the South American qualifying section: Brazil finished ten points clear of Uruguay. Now their fans will want them to match that form in the finals.

Some 16 years have passed since Brazil last reached the FIFA World Cup Final. In 2002, when Japan and Korea Republic were co-hosts, Brazil defeated Germany 2-0 in Yokohama.

GROUP E
SWITZERLAND

Switzerland enjoyed an outstanding qualifying campaign despite only reaching Russia via the play-offs. Stars such as Stephan Lichtsteiner, Xherdan Shaqiri and Granit Xhaka will be aiming to burst through the round of 16 barrier.

COACH

VLADIMIR PETKOVIĆ

Petković, 54, was born in Sarajevo in the former Yugoslavia. He played for the local club before moving to Switzerland with Chur 97, Sion, Martigny-Sports, Bellinzona, Locarno and Buochs. He then coached Swiss clubs Bellinzona, Lugano, Young Boys and Sion as well as Turkey's Samsunspor and Italy's Lazio. Petković led Lazio to victory in the *Coppa Italia* in his first season in charge in 2012-13 and then returned to Switzerland as national coach in succession to Ottmar Hitzfeld after the 2014 FIFA World Cup finals.

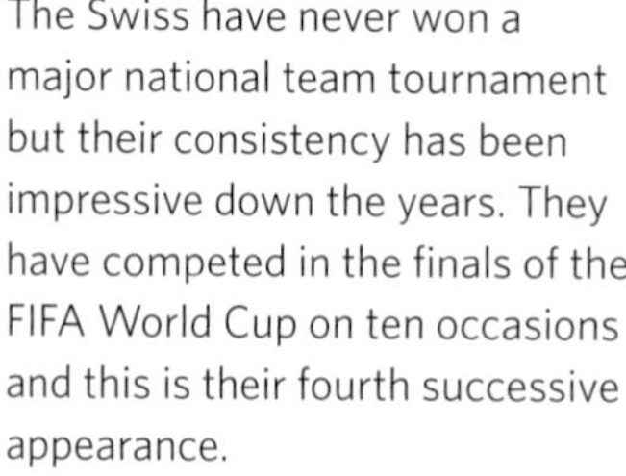

The Swiss have never won a major national team tournament but their consistency has been impressive down the years. They have competed in the finals of the FIFA World Cup on ten occasions and this is their fourth successive appearance.

Switzerland set a marker for the present generation by winning the FIFA U-17 World Cup in Nigeria in 2009. Xhaka and Ricardo Rodríguez are two of the outstanding members of that team who have fulfilled their potential at senior level and established themselves with leading clubs in Europe's biggest league competitions.

The country has always been at the forefront of world football without ever winning any senior prizes because FIFA and UEFA have their headquarters in Zurich and Nyon respectively. The history of the game in Switzerland stretches back to the 1880s, when the British helped develop the game – as evidenced in the names of major clubs such as Grasshoppers (Zurich) and Young Boys (Bern).

The *Nati* were runners-up in the 1924 Summer Olympics and then

SETTING DOWN A MARKER: Swiss players celebrate their 5-2 victory over Hungary in Basel in October 2017 which lifted them ever closer to a place in the FIFA World Cup finals, albeit they eventually needed to quality through the play-offs.

ONES TO WATCH

XHERDAN SHAQIRI

BORN: 10 October 1991
CLUB: Stoke City (England)

Shaqiri is a midfield raider who has scored 20 goals in more than 60 games for Switzerland, to where he moved with his family as a child from Kosovo. His senior debut was against Uruguay in 2010. Shaqiri scored a hat-trick against Honduras at the 2014 FIFA World Cup. He was also man of the match in a 2-1 win over Ecuador.

STEPHAN LICHTSTEINER

BORN: 16 January 1984
CLUB: Juventus (Italy)

Lichtsteiner is one of the most respected right-backs in international football through his consistently reliable displays for both his national team and Italian club Juventus. He has FIFA World Cup finals experience from 2010 and 2014 and has played more than 90 times for his country since 2005.

RECORD AT PREVIOUS TOURNAMENTS

1930	did not enter
1934	Quarter-finals
1938	Quarter-finals
1950	1st round
1954	Quarter-finals
1958	did not qualify
1962	1st round
1966	1st round
1970	did not qualify
1974	did not qualify
1978	did not qualify
1982	did not qualify
1986	did not qualify
1990	did not qualify
1994	Round of 16
1998	did not qualify
2002	did not qualify
2006	Round of 16
2010	1st round
2014	Round of 16

quarter-finalists at both the 1934 and 1938 FIFA World Cups. Stars of that era were the Abegglen brothers, Max and André, who scored more than 60 goals between them.

The man most responsible behind the scenes for this success was Karl Rappan, known as "the father of Swiss football". He devised the "Swiss Bolt" strategy, which involved using a free man at the back, a predecessor of the Italian *catenaccio* strategy using a *libero* (sweeper) in defence. Under Rappan, the Swiss reached the finals of four of the first five FIFA World Cups played after the Second World War. Their best performance was in 1954 when, as hosts, they reached the quarter-finals.

After 1966, the national side suffered a reversal of fortunes and failed to qualify for six consecutive FIFA World Cups and seven UEFA European Championships. But under English coach Roy Hodgson, they staged a comeback. They narrowly missed out on qualifying for the 1992 UEFA European Championship finals but claimed a place at the 1994 FIFA World Cup. They returned to the UEFA European finals in England two years later.

Switzerland have been a steady presence at the FIFA World Cup since 2006 and brought that experience to bear in the 2018 qualifying tournament. They won nine of their ten games in European Group B and went into the last match undefeated and leading Portugal by three points. That last match was in Lisbon, however, and the Swiss lost 2-0 to the European champions to be edged off top spot in the group table on goal difference. As runners-up, albeit only on goal difference, they were propelled into the European play-offs.

Haris Seferović was Switzerland's four-goal leading scorer in the group matches. He scored the first Swiss goal in an early 3-2 win away to Hungary, two in a 3-0 home win over Andorra and another in the subsequent victory by a similar margin away to Latvia. Seferović was unlucky in front of goal in the play-off duel with Northern Ireland, but a penalty converted by Ricardo Rodríguez, in the first leg in Belfast, was enough to separate the teams and send Switzerland to Russia.

GROUP E

COSTA RICA

The *Ticos* will be making their fifth appearance at the FIFA World Cup™ finals in Russia, and will be dreaming of emulating or even surpassing their 2014 campaign when they reached the quarter-finals.

COACH

ÓSCAR RAMÍREZ

Ramírez, 53, has a long FIFA World Cup pedigree, having been a member of the *Ticos* squad who made their finals debut in Italy in 1990. The former midfielder played 75 times for Costa Rica between 1985 and 1997 and won a string of national and international club honours with LD Alajuelense. After retiring, he was a member of the Costa Rica coaching staff at the 2006 FIFA World Cup in Germany. Ramírez guided Alajuelense to six titles and was twice named Coach of the Year before taking over the national team in succession to Paulo Wanchope in 2015.

In the group stage, Costa Rica found themselves in Group D with three former world champions in Uruguay, Italy and England. They defeated Uruguay 3-1 and Italy 1-0 before securing top spot in the table with a 0-0 draw against England. A shoot-out brought victory over Greece in the round of 16 before they fell, also on penalties, to the Netherlands in the quarter-finals.

Costa Rica maintained their momentum by reaching the quarter-finals and then the semi-finals of the 2015 and 2017 CONCACAF Gold Cup tournaments while simultaneously qualifying again for the FIFA World Cup finals.

Historians of football in Costa Rica claim that football was introduced in 1886 by a university student, Oscar Pinto Fernández, who returned home from England with a ball in his luggage. However, the introduction of the game moved forward only in 1894, when British engineers arrived to develop a tramcar system.

By the early years of the twentieth century, the game had been taken up by clubs in San José, Alajuela, Heredia and Cartago. A national governing body was founded

CHASING THE RUSSIAN DREAM: Costa Rica attacker Joel Campbell (right), one of the stars of the *Ticos'* run to the quarter-finals of the 2014 FIFA World Cup, in action against Honduras defender Henry Figueroa during their 1-1 qualifying draw in San Pedro Sula, Honduras in March 2017.

ONES TO WATCH

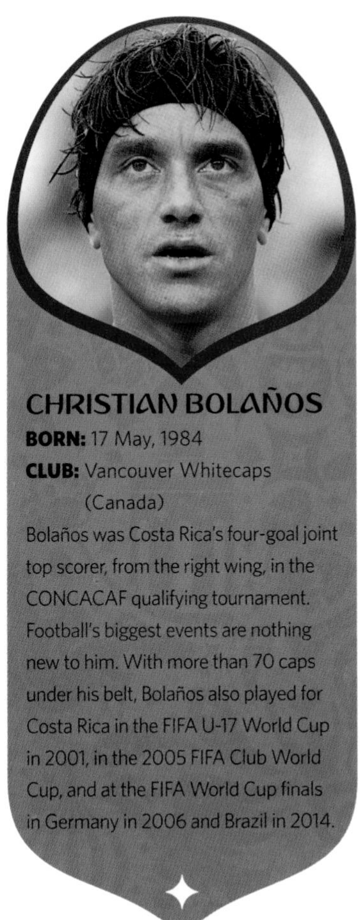

CHRISTIAN BOLAÑOS

BORN: 17 May, 1984
CLUB: Vancouver Whitecaps (Canada)

Bolaños was Costa Rica's four-goal joint top scorer, from the right wing, in the CONCACAF qualifying tournament. Football's biggest events are nothing new to him. With more than 70 caps under his belt, Bolaños also played for Costa Rica in the FIFA U-17 World Cup in 2001, in the 2005 FIFA Club World Cup, and at the FIFA World Cup finals in Germany in 2006 and Brazil in 2014.

BRYAN RUIZ

BORN: 18 August, 1985
CLUB: Sporting Lisbon (Portugal)

Ruiz is Costa Rica's captain and has played more than 100 times for his country since his debut at the CONCACAF Gold Cup in July 2005. He famously scored Costa Rica's winning goal against Italy in the FIFA World Cup finals in Brazil in 2014. He scored again against Greece in the round of 16 and converted his penalty in Costa Rica's shoot-out victory.

RECORD AT PREVIOUS TOURNAMENTS

1930	did not enter
1934	did not enter
1938	did not enter
1950	did not enter
1954	did not enter
1958	did not qualify
1962	did not qualify
1966	did not qualify
1970	did not qualify
1974	did not qualify
1978	did not qualify
1982	did not qualify
1986	did not qualify
1990	Round of 16
1994	did not qualify
1998	did not qualify
2002	1st round
2006	1st round
2010	did not qualify
2014	Quarter-finals

in 1921 as the Liga Nacional de Fútbol. The organisation went through a number of name changes before taking on its current title, Federación Costarricense de Fútbol (FEDEFUTBOL).

The first league champions were Club Sport Herediano, who are third in the all-time national rankings with 26 titles, behind Liga Deportiva Alajuelense (29) and Deportivo Saprissa (33).

Costa Rica's national team have a proud record in regional competition. They won the inaugural central American championship in 1941 and then on a further six occasions before the creation of the regional governing body CONCACAF. Costa Rica won the inaugural CONCACAF Championship in 1991 and had two more victories before finishing joint-third last year in what has now become the CONCACAF Gold Cup.

The *Ticos*' status in central America also earned invitations to guest at the *Copa América* on five occasions. They reached the quarter-finals in both 2001 and 2004 and were eliminated in the first round in the centenary edition *(Centenario)* of the *Copa América* in the United States in 2016.

By now, Costa Rica's players had established reputations far beyond their own borders. Goalkeeper Keylor Navas became the first Costa Rican player to win the UEFA Champions League with Real Madrid, while defenders Michael Umaña, Johnny Acosta, Giancarlo González and Cristian Gamboa, midfielders Celso Borges and Randall Azofeifa as well as forwards Bryan Ruiz and Christian Bolaños have now all topped a half-century of international appearances.

Costa Rica's high ranking in CONCACAF meant they did not enter the 2018 FIFA World Cup Russia qualifying competition until the fourth round, where they topped a mini-league featuring Panama, Haiti and Jamaica to reach the concluding fifth round, a six-team round-robin with Honduras, Mexico, Panama, Trinidad & Tobago and the USA.

Here they lost only twice to secure a finals place by finishing runners-up behind Mexico and ahead of Panama, with Honduras taking the play-off slot.

GROUP E

SERBIA

Serbia are flying to the FIFA World Cup™ finals for the fourth time since the break-up of the former Yugoslavia. Their talent has never been in doubt and they proved their resilience by topping a tough qualifying group.

COACH

MLADEN KRSTAJIĆ

Krstajić, 44, took over as national team coach from Slavoljub Muslin after the completion of the FIFA World Cup qualifying campaign. The former central defender had played for Serbia at the finals in Germany in 2006. At club level, he won three league titles and the domestic cup with Partizan and a German league and cup double with Werder Bremen. Krstajić totalled 59 appearances, with two goals, for Serbia between 1999 and 2008. After retiring he became technical director of Partizan before later joining the national team coaching staff.

The image of Yugoslavia as the "Argentina of Europe" was fostered back in 1930 when they were one of only four European nations to brave the Atlantic sea crossing and attend the first FIFA World Cup finals in Uruguay.

Exports back then included inside forward Ivan Bek, who played for FC Sète 34 in France. Bek scored one goal in a 2-1 defeat of Brazil, which put Yugoslavia in the semi-finals. Other key players were forwards Aleksandar Tirnanić and Branislav "Bane" Sekulić, both of whom were later national team managers.

Yugoslavia returned to the finals without success in 1950 despite a squad full of future managerial talent, including Ivan "Ivica" Horvat, Zlatko "Čik" Čajkowski, Bernard "Bajdo" Vukas, Stjepan Bobek and Rajko Mitić. Beaten in the quarter-finals by West Germany in both 1954 and 1958, they achieved their best finish in 1962, when they finished fourth in Chile.

In the UEFA European Championship, Yugoslavia were runners-up in the first tournament in 1960 and then again in 1968, while Red Star Belgrade, one of the

KEEPING THE FANS HAPPY: Aleksandar Mitrović (right) is joined by Aleksandar Prijović after he had scored Serbia's equalising goal in a 1-1 draw at home to Wales in the Rajko Mitić Stadium in European Group D in Belgrade last June.

ONES TO WATCH

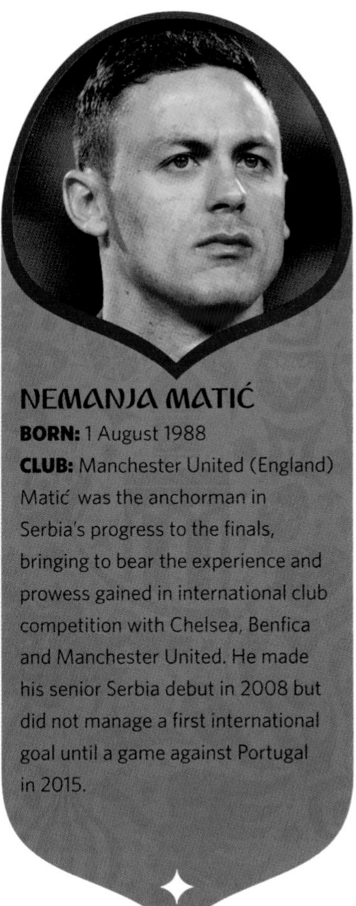

NEMANJA MATIĆ

BORN: 1 August 1988

CLUB: Manchester United (England)

Matić was the anchorman in Serbia's progress to the finals, bringing to bear the experience and prowess gained in international club competition with Chelsea, Benfica and Manchester United. He made his senior Serbia debut in 2008 but did not manage a first international goal until a game against Portugal in 2015.

ALEKSANDAR KOLAROV

BORN: 10 November 1985

CLUB: Roma (Italy)

Kolarov, an experienced left-back and centre-back, has been rejuvenated since his transfer to Roma last year. The former Serbian Footballer of the Year has played more than 70 times for his country since his debut a decade ago. At club level, he has won trophies in Italy and England with Lazio and Manchester City.

RECORD AT PREVIOUS TOURNAMENTS

1930	Semi-finals
1934	did not qualify
1938	did not qualify
1950	1st round
1954	Quarter-finals
1958	Quarter-finals
1962	4th place
1966	did not qualify
1970	did not qualify
1974	2nd round
1978	did not qualify
1982	1st round
1986	did not qualify
1990	Quarter-finals
1994	suspended
1998	Round of 16
2002	did not qualify
2006	1st round
2010	1st round
2014	did not qualify

country's two leading clubs along with Partizan, won the Champions Cup in 1990-91 and was runners-up in the 1978-79 UEFA Cup before Yugoslavia broke up in the early 1990s. Serbia & Montenegro emerged and reorganised effectively enough for the national team to reach the finals of 1998 FIFA World Cup in France. New heroes such as Dejan Savićević, Predrag Mijatović and Sinisa Mihajlović led them as far as the second round.

They qualified again, in 2006 and 2010, albeit without progressing beyond the first round.

Now they return to the finals after heading European qualifying Group D. They ended the campaign two points clear of the Republic of Ireland after a testing competitive campaign also featuring Wales, who were UEFA EURO semi-finalists in 2016, and old rivals Austria as well as Georgia and Moldova.

Important results as the campaign ran on included a 1-1 draw away to Wales in Cardiff with a late goal from Aleksandar Mitrović, then a 1-0 win against the Irish in Dublin. This win, as the final table proved, was crucial, with Aleksandar Kolarov scoring the only goal ten minutes into the second half. Ultimately, Serbia needed to defeat Georgia in Belgrade to clinch top spot, whatever might have happened in the other simultaneous last match between Wales and the Republic of Ireland.

There was no need for complicated mathematics, however as Serbia won on the night and overall courtesy of the relief of a 74th-minute strike from Aleksandar Prijović. Mitrović ended as leading marksman with six goals, followed by Dusan Tadić on four and then Kolarov, Filip Kostić and Mijat Gaćinović with two each. Prijović scored only once – but his solitary strike proved even more important than all the rest.

The Serbs thus finished clear of the Irish, with Wales third ahead of Austria, Georgia and Moldova. They were also the 20-goal leading scorers in the group to underline their right to a place back in the FIFA World Cup finals after having finished third behind Belgium and Croatia in the vain qualifying campaign for a place in the finals four years ago in Brazil.

GROUP F

GERMANY

Germany will be defending, in Russia, not only their status as world champions but a magnificent all-time record in the FIFA World Cup™. They have been champions four times since their first triumph in 1954.

COACH

JOACHIM LÖW

Joachim "Jogi" Löw, 58, was Jürgen Klinsmann's assistant when Germany finished third at the 2006 FIFA World Cup and succeeded him as coach afterwards. Previously he had bossed Stuttgart, Fenerbahce, Karlsruhe, Adanaspor, Tirol Innsbruck and FK Austria. He used a blend of technique and physical power to take Germany to the EURO 2008 Final, then introduced a string of talented new youngsters on the way to the semi-finals of the 2010 FIFA World Cup, the semi-finals of UEFA EURO 2012 and FIFA World Cup victory in Brazil in 2014.

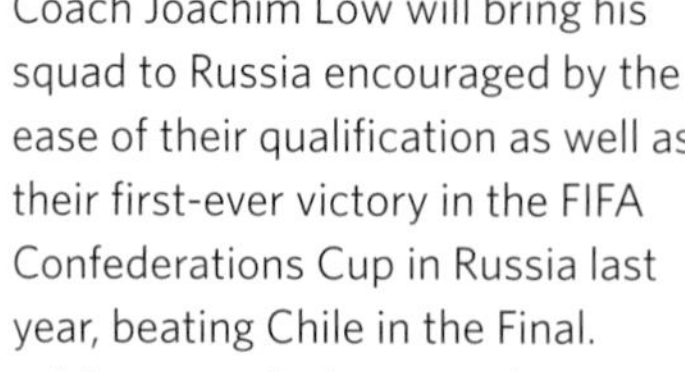

Coach Joachim Löw will bring his squad to Russia encouraged by the ease of their qualification as well as their first-ever victory in the FIFA Confederations Cup in Russia last year, beating Chile in the Final.

Löw was missing a number of senior players, but the team defeated Australia and Cameroon and drew with Chile in the first round before defeating Mexico in the semi-finals and then the South American champions, 1-0 at the second attempt, in the final. Borussia Mönchengladbach's Lars Stindl scored the winner.

Success in Russia came amid a commanding performance in the FIFA World Cup qualifiers. Germany won all of their ten matches in European Group C against Northern Ireland, Czech Republic, Norway, Azerbaijan and San Marino. They were the only European nation to complete the preliminary section with a 100% record, scoring 43 goals and conceding four.

That demonstration of attacking penetration and defensive security saw Germany top the table with 30 points, 11 clear of Northern Ireland. Their most decisive victory was 8-0

CELEBRATION TIME: Germany's captain Julian Draxler and his team-mates hoist the trophy aloft in celebration after they had defeated Chile 1-0, thanks to a goal from Lars Stindl, in last year's FIFA Confederations Cup final in Saint Petersburg.

ONES TO WATCH

THOMAS MÜLLER

BORN: 13 September 1989

CLUB: Bayern Munich

Müller is the latest forward of that name to intimidate rivals around the penalty box. The Bayern academy product crowned his first senior season in 2009-10 by winning both the Golden Boot (with five goals) and Best Young Player at the 2010 FIFA World Cup. His five goals made him the second-highest scorer when Germany won the title four years later.

TONI KROOS

BORN: 4 January 1990

CLUB: Real Madrid (Spain)

Kroos, born in the former East Germany shortly before reunification, made his name with Bayern Munich. The midfielder also had a loan spell at Bayer Leverkusen before joining Real Madrid after anchoring Germany to win the FIFA World Cup in 2014. With Madrid he has won the UEFA Champions League twice, along with two FIFA Club World Cups.

RECORD AT PREVIOUS TOURNAMENTS

1930	did not enter
1934	3rd place
1938	1st round
1950	did not enter
1954	CHAMPIONS
1958	4th place
1962	Quarter-finals
1966	Runners-up
1970	3rd place
1974	CHAMPIONS
1978	2nd round
1982	Runners-up
1986	Runners-up
1990	CHAMPIONS
1994	Quarter-finals
1998	Quarter-finals
2002	Runners-up
2006	3rd place
2010	3rd place
2014	CHAMPIONS

away to San Marino with a hat-trick from midfielder Serge Gnabry and a double from wing-back Jonas Hector.

It was not until their fifth game, in Azerbaijan, that Germany conceded a goal, and that was in a 4-1 victory. A subsequent 3-1 victory over Northern Ireland in Belfast secured the holders' flight back to the finals with one matchday to spare. Thomas Müller and Sandro Wagner were Germany's leading scorers followed by Gnabry, Leon Goretzka, Timo Werner and Julian Draxler with three each. Goretzka, Werner and Draxler were all members of the Confederations Cup squad when captain Draxler was voted player of the tournament.

Germany's proud record in the FIFA World Cup goes back to a third-place finish in 1934 and their first victory in 1954, when coach Sepp Herberger's team defeated favourites Hungary 3-2 in a final that became known as the *Wunder von Bern* (Miracle of Berne). Victory made legends of stars such as brothers Fritz and Ottmar Walter and Helmut Rahn, who scored the winning goal.

From then on, the Germans only grew in stature. They were semi-finalists in 1958, quarter-finalists in 1962 and runners-up in 1966, when a team captained by Uwe Seeler and featuring a new talent in Franz Beckenbauer lost 4-2 to hosts England after extra time.

The mid-1970s belonged to the Germans at both national and club level. Beckenbauer's Bayern Munich won a hat-trick of UEFA European Cups in 1974, 1975 and 1976 and provided the nucleus of the national side that won the FIFA World Cup in 1974 as well as the UEFA European Championship in 1972 and 1980.

Beckenbauer revolutionised the sweeper's role into one of attack as well as defence while Gerd Müller scored 68 goals in 62 internationals. Later heroes included Karl-Heinz Rummenigge, Lothar Matthäus, Rudi Völler, Jürgen Klinsmann, Thomas Hässler and Matthias Sammer.

In 1990, Germany again enjoyed FIFA World Cup success, and following reunification they were able to capitalise on their new-found resources to win UEFA EURO 96. That was their last senior title until four years ago at the Maracaña.

GROUP F

MEXICO

Mexico return to Russia determined to build on the experience and positive impression created by *El Tri* when coach Juan Carlos Osorio led them to the semi-finals of last year's FIFA Confederations Cup.

COACH

JUAN CARLOS OSORIO

Osorio, 56, a Colombian, took up his first national team role when he was appointed by Mexico in 2015 in succession to Miguel Herrera and Ricardo Ferretti. As a midfielder, Osorio had played for Deportivo Pereira and Chicago Fire before going into coaching as an assistant for five years with Manchester City. Later came spells in charge at Millonarios of Bogotá, then Chicago Fire and New York Red Bulls before he returned home with Once Caldas and Atlético Nacional. With the latter, he won six Colombian domestic trophies in four years.

Only four nations (Brazil, Germany, Italy and Argentina) have appeared in the finals more often than Mexico, who have brought their technically accomplished style to the big stage on 16 occasions. One of the original finalists, Mexico have missed out since then only five times.

Their proudest performances were in 1970 and 1986 when, as hosts each time, they reached the quarter-finals. Last time out, in Brazil, they came close to emulating those achievements. In the round of 16 in Fortaleza, *El Tri* led the Netherlands 1-0 with two minutes of normal time remaining, only to lose 2-1 in stoppage time.

Mexico have maintained their momentum ever since. They won the CONCACAF Gold Cup in 2015 for the seventh time, reached the quarter-finals of the *Copa América Centenario* in 2016 and then the semi-finals last year of both the FIFA Confederations Cup and the Gold Cup again.

Key players along the way have been penalty-saving goalkeeper Guillermo Ochoa, veteran skipper Rafael Márquez, defenders Miguel Layún and Héctor Moreno,

ENJOYING THE MOMENT: Goalkeeper Guillermo Ochoa of Mexico is in celebratory mood during the FIFA Confederations Cup in Russia last year when *El Tri* reached the semi-finals before losing to eventual tournament winners Germany.

ONES TO WATCH

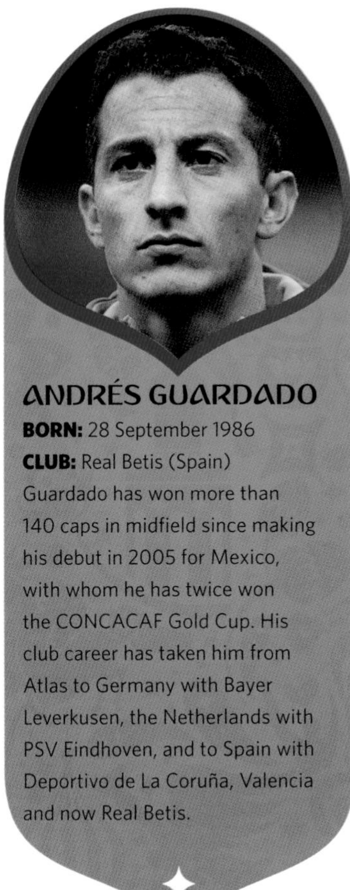

ANDRÉS GUARDADO

BORN: 28 September 1986
CLUB: Real Betis (Spain)
Guardado has won more than 140 caps in midfield since making his debut in 2005 for Mexico, with whom he has twice won the CONCACAF Gold Cup. His club career has taken him from Atlas to Germany with Bayer Leverkusen, the Netherlands with PSV Eindhoven, and to Spain with Deportivo de La Coruña, Valencia and now Real Betis.

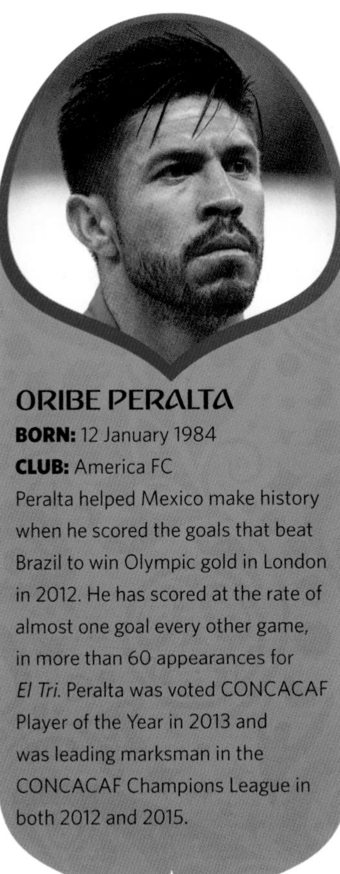

ORIBE PERALTA

BORN: 12 January 1984
CLUB: America FC
Peralta helped Mexico make history when he scored the goals that beat Brazil to win Olympic gold in London in 2012. He has scored at the rate of almost one goal every other game, in more than 60 appearances for *El Tri*. Peralta was voted CONCACAF Player of the Year in 2013 and was leading marksman in the CONCACAF Champions League in both 2012 and 2015.

RECORD AT PREVIOUS TOURNAMENTS

1930	1st round
1934	did not qualify
1938	withdrew
1950	1st round
1954	1st round
1958	1st round
1962	1st round
1966	1st round
1970	Quarter-finals
1974	did not qualify
1978	1st round
1982	did not qualify
1986	Quarter-finals
1990	disqualified
1994	1st round
1998	1st round
2002	1st round
2006	1st round
2010	1st round
2014	Round of 16

midfielders Andrés Guardado and Carlos Vela, and forwards Javier "Chicharito" Hernández, Oribe Peralta and Giovani dos Santos. Peralta was the two-goal hero of Mexico's Olympic triumph in 2012 while Hernández is *El Tri*'s all-time record marksman with around 50 goals to his name.

Mexico joined the CONCACAF qualifying section for 2018 at the fourth-round stage. They had no problems topping Group A ahead of Honduras, Canada and El Salvador, winning five of their six games and drawing the other to finish eight points clear of Honduras.

The fifth round was the traditional, final six-team group. Mexico began it in perfect style with a 2-1 win away to the United States in Columbus, Ohio. Layún opened the scoring and Márquez struck the winner two minutes from the end. A goalless draw in Panama followed before Mexico embarked on a run of three victories followed by a goalless home draw against the US, which put them in command of the section.

Ultimately, a 1-0 win over Panama on 1 September 2017 saw Mexico become only the fourth nation to clinch qualification for the finals (after Brazil, IR Iran and Japan) and with three matches remaining. Hirving Lozano, a winger for PSV Eindhoven, struck the decisive goal at the Estadio Azteca in Mexico City.

With five goals, Lozano was the team's leading marksman in the campaign. He began his career with Pachuca, one of the cradles of football in Mexico. The game was introduced there by tin miners Cornwall in southwest England to the state of Hidalgo at the start of the last century.

Star players down the years since then have included goalkeeper Antonio Carvajal, Claudio Suárez, Jorge Campos and Hugo Sanchez.

Carvajal was one of only two players to appear at five FIFA World Cups, in his case between 1950 in Brazil and 1966 in England. Suárez, nicknamed "El Emperador", remains Mexico's record international after 177 caps between 1992 and 2006. Campos was a star goalkeeper who could also play in attack, while free-scoring Hugo Sanchez was a star at both Atlético and Real Madrid.

GROUP F

SWEDEN

Sweden have a proud FIFA World Cup™ record after finishing third on two occasions. Though they missed out on the last two finals tournaments, they have proved their worth by beating Italy in the European play-offs.

COACH

JAN OLOF "Janne" ANDERSSON

Andersson, 55, took over as national manager in 2016 from Erik Hamrén after Sweden were eliminated in the first round of the finals of the UEFA European Championship. Previously, Andersson had coached Halmstad, Orgryte and Norrköping. He was voted Coach of the Year in 2004 after leading Halmstad to second place in the Swedish championship. He celebrated his first league title win with Norrköping in 2015. Andersson had spent almost all his playing career with Alets IK, for whom he became their all-time leading scorer.

This represented a victory for team spirit, organisation, commitment and the shrewd management of national coach Jan Olof "Janne" Andersson. He has been in command for only two years but has had to rebuild his team in a new image since the international retirement of Zlatan Ibrahimović after the UEFA European Championship in 2016.

The immediate challenge was a testing qualifying group that included France and the Netherlands, who had been quarter- and semi-finalists respectively at the finals in Brazil in 2014. France were decisive winners of the group while Sweden and the Netherlands ended up level on points, Andersson's men edging second place and a play-offs slot on goal difference.

The two decisive matches in the group were the first and the last games against the Dutch. The opening clash ended in a 1-1 draw in Solna, with a first-half goal from Sweden's Marcus Berg being cancelled out by a second-half equaliser from Wesley Sneijder. The return was played in Amsterdam on the last matchday. The Dutch had to win by seven goals to pull level on points and turn around the goals tallies, but in the end they

FIFA WORLD CUP™ PARTY TIME: Sweden's players wave to their fans and families in Milan after holding out for the 0-0 draw away to Italy which was enough to send them to the finals in Russia, 1-0 on aggregate, in the European play-offs.

ONES TO WATCH

SEBASTIAN LARSSON

BORN: 6 June 1985

CLUB: Hull City (England)

Larsson, with more than 90 international appearances to his credit, has been a mainstay of the Swedish attack and midfield since 2008, when he made his debut in a friendly against Turkey. From Eskilstuna, he has played all his senior football in England with Arsenal, Birmingham City, Sunderland and now Hull City, whom he joined last summer.

ANDREAS GRANQVIST

BORN: 16 April 1985

CLUB: Krasnodar (Russia)

Granqvist is one of the few "visiting" players at the FIFA World Cup to have the advantage of knowing the local conditions thanks to his Russian league experience with Krasnodar. He has also played for Helsingborgs, Wigan Athletic, Groningen and Genoa. A solid defender, he was named national team captain in 2016. His FIFA World Cup qualifying exploits helped him win Swedish Player of the Year in 2017.

RECORD AT PREVIOUS TOURNAMENTS

1930	did not enter
1934	Quarter-finals
1938	4th place
1950	3rd place
1954	did not qualify
1958	Runners-up
1962	did not qualify
1966	did not qualify
1970	1st round
1974	2nd round
1978	1st round
1982	did not qualify
1986	did not qualify
1990	1st round
1994	3rd place
1998	did not qualify
2002	Round of 16
2006	Round of 16
2010	did not qualify
2014	did not qualify

won "only" 2-0. Berg finished the campaign as their eight-goal leading scorer.

The play-off draw matched Sweden with Italy. Another difficult task, but yet again it was mission accomplished. Andersson's men won 1-0 at home with a goal from AEK Athens midfielder Jakob Johansson, and then held out heroically at Milan's Stadio Giuseppe Meazza for probably the most famous goalless draw in Swedish football history. Goalkeeper Robin Olsson and skipper Andreas Granqvist, at the heart of defence, played the games of their lives.

Sweden thus headed for the finals by underlining their status, down the years, as Scandinavia's top national side. The Swedish Football Association was formed in 1904 and joined FIFA the same year. The national side made their debut in 1908 and entered the first four Olympic tournaments with mixed success. This era produced the country's first great striker in Sven Rydell, who scored 49 goals in 43 games.

Their FIFA World Cup progress was relentless, however. They were quarter-finalists in 1934, fourth in 1938, third in 1950 and runners-up as hosts to Pelé's Brazil in 1958. In between, Sweden were also Olympic champions in 1948, when they produced more great forwards in Gunnar Gren, Gunnar Nordahl and Nils Liedholm – the legendary "Gre-No-Li" trio – and the flying wingers Kurt Hamrin and Karl Lennart "Nacka" Skoglund.

A decline followed in the 1960s, but Sweden qualified for all three FIFA World Cup tournaments in the 1970s, with central defender Björn Nordqvist clocking up a then record 115 appearances between 1963 and 1978. By now Sweden's clubs were making an impact in international competition as well. Malmö reached the UEFA European Champions Cup final in 1979 while IFK Göteborg won the UEFA Cup twice, in 1982 and 1987.

Sweden's first appearance in the European Championship finals came in 1992, by virtue of being hosts, but they were beaten in the semi-finals by Germany. They followed up by finishing third at the 1994 FIFA World Cup in the USA, with a fine team starring goalkeeper Thomas Ravelli, Jonas Thern and Tomas Brolin.

GROUP F

KOREA REPUBLIC

Korea Republic made Asian football history by reaching the semi-finals of the 2002 FIFA World Cup™, which the nation co-hosted with Japan. Matching that achievement remains the inspiration for the coaching staff and players.

COACH

SHIN TAE-YONG

Shin, 49, took over the Korea Republic national team in June last year from former German international Uli Stielike. Previously he had guided Seongnam Ilhwa Chunma to victory in the 2010 AFC Champions League. In 2014, he was appointed caretaker manager of the national team and was later handed charge of the U-23 and then U-20 teams. As a player, Shin was an attacking midfielder with Ilhwa Chunma and Queensland Roar. He scored three goals in 23 appearances for the senior national team between 1992 and 1997.

Korean players from the south of the peninsula had first made their mark on the international stage by reaching the finals in Switzerland in 1954, six years after the country gained independence from Japan. Continuing to play a leading role in the development of Asian international football in the east, they won the initial two Asian Championships in 1956 and 1960.

For two decades, the domestic game marked time until the creation of a professional league was rewarded with regular appearances at the finals of successive FIFA World Cups from 1986 onwards. Key players in the late 1990s were Hong Myung-bo, a powerful central defender, and the German-based Cha Bum-kun, whose son Cha Du-ri would emulate him as a FIFA World Cup footballer.

A further decisive step forward came in 1996 when the country was awarded co-hosting rights with Japan to stage the 2002 finals. Dutch coach Guus Hiddink was appointed national manager at the start of 2001 and worked a minor footballing miracle. Roared on by their passionate supporters, the

HEADING FOR THE FINALS: Son Heung-Min (7) of hosts Korea Republic celebrates with Ki Sung-Yueng and substitute Hwang Ui-Jo (10) after scoring one of the Reds' eight goals against Laos in their FIFA World Cup Asian second round qualifying tie in Hwaseong.

ONES TO WATCH

SON HEUNG-MIN

BORN: 8 July 1992

CLUB: Tottenham Hotspur (England)

Son has proved hugely popular with fans of Hamburg, Bayer Leverkusen and Tottenham Hotspur since making his name as a teenage forward with FC Seoul. He played at the 2014 FIFA World Cup and helped Korea finish runners-up at the 2015 AFC Asian Cup. On joining Spurs for £22m in 2015, he became Asia's most expensive player.

LEE DONG-GOOK

BORN: 29 April 1979

CLUB: Jeonbuk Hyundai Motors (Korea Republic)

Lee is Korea Republic's most experienced star, with more than 30 goals in a century of international appearances. Lee is also a leading marksman in the domestic K-League and has had spells in Europe with Werder Bremen and Middlesbrough. He was a member of the Korean squad at the 1998 and 2010 FIFA World Cups.

RECORD AT PREVIOUS TOURNAMENTS

1930	did not exist
1934	did not exist
1938	did not exist
1950	did not enter
1954	1st round
1958	entry refused
1962	did not qualify
1966	did not enter
1970	did not qualify
1974	did not qualify
1978	did not qualify
1982	did not qualify
1986	1st round
1990	1st round
1994	1st round
1998	1st round
2002	4th place
2006	1st round
2010	Round of 16
2014	1st round

Koreans defeated Poland 2-0, played out a 1-1 draw with the United States and then beat Portugal 1-0 to progress beyond the group stage.

Victories over Italy and Spain earned them a place in history as the only Asian nation to reach the FIFA World Cup semi-finals, and they duly finished a proud fourth.

Following up on that feat has proved challenging. The furthest the Koreans have progressed since 2002 has been the round of 16 in South Africa in 2010, when they were eliminated 2-1 by Uruguay. In other competitions, the Koreans have prospered: they can point to four successes in the Asian Games - most recently in 2014; a hat-trick in the EAFF East Asian Cup in 2003, 2008 and 2015; and a bronze medal at the 2012 Summer Olympics in London.

The eight-group qualifying competition for the 2018 FIFA World Cup doubled up with that of the 2019 AFC Asian Cup. Progressing from the second round was not a problem. Korea Republic won all seven games, home and away, with 27 goals to their credit and none conceded by goalkeeper Kim Seung-gyu and deputies Kwoun Sun-tae and Kim Jin-hyeon. Tottenham's Son Heung-min scored a hat-trick in an 8-0 defeat of Laos.

They should have played Kuwait in their last game, but this never took place. Kuwait forfeited the match after having been suspended from FIFA membership, and the tie was awarded 3-0 to Korea Republic.

They began their third-round campaign with victories over China PR and Qatar and a goalless draw with Syria on neutral territory. Defeats by IR Iran in October 2016, then China PR and Qatar in the spring of 2017, saw them sitting second in the group, seven points behind IR Iran, who had already qualified, and one ahead of Uzbekistan.

Under Shin Tae-yong, Korea Republic achieved goalless draws at home to IR Iran and away to Uzbekistan, which secured the runners-up spot and their place in Russia. Son Heung-min was the *Reds'* leading scorer in qualifying with seven goals, followed by Ki Sung-yueng and Koo Ja-cheol (four each). Hence the *Reds* are into the finals for the ninth successive time.

GROUP G

BELGIUM

Belgium return to the FIFA World Cup™ finals with a refreshed national team fulfilling their historic status: *Les Diables Rouges*, or *Red Devils*, were among the four European nations at the initial finals in 1930.

COACH

ROBERTO MARTÍNEZ

Martínez, 44, is a former Spanish midfielder who has been in charge of the Belgian national team since succeeding Marc Wilmots in the summer of 2016. He began his playing career at Real Zaragoza, with whom he won the *Copa del Rey*, and moved to England to join Wigan Athletic in 1995. Later he played for Motherwell, Walsall and Swansea City, whose manager he became in 2007. In 2013 he guided Wigan to FA Cup victory and then moved to Everton, before stepping into the arena of national teams with the *Red Devils*.

On that occasion, Belgium were eliminated in the first round group stage after defeats by the United States and Paraguay. However, their most recent appearance was far more successful as Marc Wilmots's squad reached the quarter-finals in Brazil four years ago.

The Belgian Football Association was founded in 1895, created the second-oldest league outside Great Britain, and was one of the pioneering forces behind the formation of FIFA in 1904.

Subsequently, the amateur nature of the Belgian domestic game hindered progress in terms of both domestic development and national team results. Amateurism was only formally discarded in 1972, and the introduction of professionalism saw results immediately improve.

Belgium appeared at the FIFA World Cup finals on only two occasions between the 1950s and 1980s. However, between 1972 and 1984 they reached the last eight of four successive UEFA European Championships, finishing as runners-up to West Germany in Italy in 1980.

The class of 1980 represented Belgium for almost a decade and

COMING TO THE RESCUE: Centre-forward Romelu Lukaku expresses his delight and relief after scoring Belgium's last-minute equaliser in the 1-1 home draw against Greece at the King Baudouin Stadium in Brussels in March 2017. It was the only game the Belgians failed to win as they dominated qualifying Group H.

ONES TO WATCH

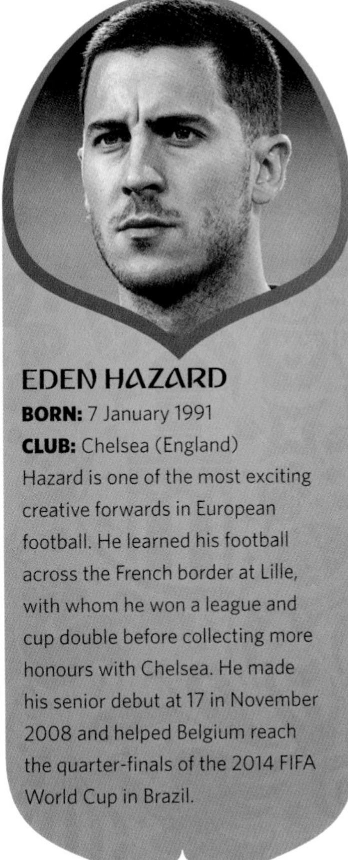

EDEN HAZARD

BORN: 7 January 1991

CLUB: Chelsea (England)

Hazard is one of the most exciting creative forwards in European football. He learned his football across the French border at Lille, with whom he won a league and cup double before collecting more honours with Chelsea. He made his senior debut at 17 in November 2008 and helped Belgium reach the quarter-finals of the 2014 FIFA World Cup in Brazil.

ROMELU LUKAKU

BORN: 13 May 1993

CLUB: Manchester United (England)

Lukaku made headlines around Europe as a teenage centre-forward with his initial goalscoring exploits for Anderlecht. He has already played more than 50 times for Belgium since making his debut in 2010. Lukaku joined Manchester United from Everton last year for a club record £75m after spells with Chelsea and West Bromwich Albion.

RECORD AT PREVIOUS TOURNAMENTS

1930	1st round
1934	1st round
1938	1st round
1950	withdrew
1954	1st round
1958	did not qualify
1962	did not qualify
1966	did not qualify
1970	1st round
1974	did not qualify
1978	did not qualify
1982	2nd round
1986	Fourth place
1990	Round of 16
1994	Round of 16
1998	1st round
2002	Round of 16
2006	did not qualify
2010	did not qualify
2014	Quarter-finals

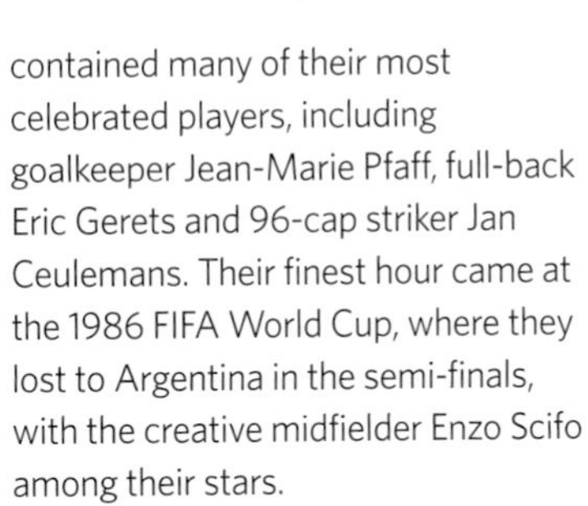

contained many of their most celebrated players, including goalkeeper Jean-Marie Pfaff, full-back Eric Gerets and 96-cap striker Jan Ceulemans. Their finest hour came at the 1986 FIFA World Cup, where they lost to Argentina in the semi-finals, with the creative midfielder Enzo Scifo among their stars.

Fourth place marked the Belgians' best-ever FIFA World Cup. It was also the second of six successive appearances at the finals. Belgium missed out in 2006 and 2010 but returned in Brazil four years ago with a team refashioned by Wilmots around a rising new generation of highly talented youngsters.

Wilmots left after Belgium reached the quarter-finals of the UEFA European Championship in France in 2016. His work has been carried on by Roberto Martínez, only the second foreign coach since the late 1950s.

Chelsea's Thibaut Courtois has established himself as one of the most commanding goalkeepers in Europe. English Premier League stalwarts Toby Alderweireld and Jan Vertonghen from Tottenham Hotspur have brought back a defensive consistency, that Belgium has lacked since the 1980s and the days of Eric Gerets and Walter Meeuws.

In midfield, Martínez has been spoiled for choice with the likes of Axel Witsel and England-based Marouane Fellaini, Nacer Chadli, Mousa Dembélé and Kevin De Bruyne. De Bruyne's outstanding performances for Manchester City over the past two seasons have established him as one of the finest modern midfielders anywhere in the world game.

Belgium boast a balanced attack with Eden Hazard and Dries Mertens creating openings for Romelu Lukaku and/or Divock Origi as well as Michy Batshuayi and Christian Benteke.

Martínez's men launched their qualifying campaign positively, with 21 goals in four victories over Cyprus, Bosnia-Herzegovina, Gibraltar and Estonia before being held 1-1 at home by Greece. Those were the only points dropped. Belgium won their next five games to finish nine points ahead of the Greeks atop the final table for European Group H.

Lukaku was the qualifying group's top scorer with 11 goals, while Hazard claimed six.

GROUP G

PANAMA

Panama will be appearing at the FIFA World Cup™ finals for the first time in their history after a dramatic climax to the qualifying campaign, rewarded by the government declaring a national holiday.

COACH

HERNÁN DARÍO GÓMEZ

Gómez, 62, is a Colombian who guided his home nation to France 1998 and Ecuador to the Republic of Korea/Japan in 2002. His success with debutants Panama is even more impressive. Gómez played for Independiente and Atlético Nacional of Medellín before his career was cut short by a knee injury. He was assistant coach to Francisco Maturana with Colombia at the 1990 and 1994 FIFA World Cups, then led Atlético Nacional to the domestic league title. He coached Colombia, Ecuador and Guatemala before taking up a fourth national team role with Panama in 2014.

For many years, Panama, where baseball is so popular, was considered one of the least strong footballing nations in Central America. A football association was created in 1937 in time for the national team to make their competitive debut at Panama's hosting of the Central American and Caribbean Games the following year.

Their only trophy success arrived in 1951 when, as hosts, they won the regional championship by topping a three-nation mini-league. They had stood aside from the FIFA World Cup qualifying competition for the finals in Brazil the previous year and remained on the sidelines for the next two decades.

Finally, on 4 April 1976, Panama played their first FIFA World Cup qualifying tie. Now, 94 ties and 11 tournaments later, they go to the finals for the first time courtesy of the United States' home defeat by Trinidad & Tobago and a late goal from Román Torres, which defeated Costa Rica.

The journey launched by old heroes led by "Cascarita" Tapia is now being completed by a new generation led by the likes of Blas Pérez, Gabriel and Román Torres,

MAKING FIFA WORLD CUP™ HISTORY: Panama's Anibal Godoy in ecstasy after he and his team-mates had qualified for the FIFA World Cup finals for the first time in his country's history courtesy of a 2-1 home win over Costa Rica in Panama City last October.

ONES TO WATCH

GABRIEL GÓMEZ

BORN: 29 May 1984

CLUB: Atlético Bucaramanga (Colombia)

Midfielder Gómez is Panama's most-capped international with more than 140 appearances to his name since he made his debut in 2003. He has played club football in Panama, Colombia, Portugal, Cyprus, Mexico, the United States and Costa Rica. Gómez was a key figure in the Panama team who took third place in the 2015 CONCACAF Gold Cup.

BLAS PÉREZ

BORN: 13 March 1981

CLUB: Municipal (Guatemala)

Pérez made his debut for Panama in 2001 and is among the country's record marksmen with more than 40 goals. His goalscoring career has taken him to Uruguay, Colombia, Spain, Mexico, the United Arab Emirates, the United States, Canada, Bolivia and now Guatemala. He described qualification as "the most beautiful moment" of his 16-year career in the national team.

RECORD AT PREVIOUS TOURNAMENTS

1930	did not enter
1934	did not enter
1938	did not enter
1950	did not enter
1954	did not enter
1958	did not enter
1962	did not enter
1966	did not enter
1970	did not enter
1974	did not enter
1978	did not qualify
1982	did not qualify
1986	did not qualify
1990	did not qualify
1994	did not qualify
1998	did not qualify
2002	did not qualify
2006	did not qualify
2010	did not qualify
2014	did not qualify

Luis Tejada, Jaime Penedo, Felipe Baloy and Gabriel Gómez.

Panama competed in the 1978 qualifying competition out of concern that their FIFA membership might be at risk if they maintained their long-running absence; they had joined world football's governing body in 1938.

After warm-ups against club teams, Panama defeated Costa Rica 3-2 in front of a 7,000-strong crowd in the Estadio Revolución, now the Estadio Rommel Fernández. "Cascarita" Tapia was the only professional; all of his team-mates played in Panama's regional leagues. He was one of the goalscorers along with Federico Ponce and Agustin Sanchez, but other results went against them.

It took Panama another 16 years to beat Costa Rica again. Then a team containing some of Panama's finest – brothers Jorge and Julio Dely Valdés, Rommel Fernández and René Mendieta – defeated the *Ticos* 2-1. Some 25 years later, a further victory over Costa Rica has been rewarded with Panama's most important step forward.

The top six CONCACAF teams in the FIFA/Coca-Cola World Ranking were seeded directly to the fourth round of 2018 qualifying. Panama finished runners-up in Group B to Costa Rica and were thus propelled into the concluding six-team group.

They opened brightly with a win in Honduras and a home draw with Mexico. Further draws followed at home to the USA and away to Costa Rica before they arrived at the last matchday needing to beat already-qualified Costa Rica and needing the United States to lose away to Trinidad & Tobago, who could not qualify.

That was how it played out. In Panama City, Costa Rica led 1-0 at half-time. Then Lausanne forward Blas Pérez equalised shortly after the interval and Seattle Sounders defender Román Torres scored the winner two minutes from time. Simultaneously the USA lost 2-1.

Panama thus clinched the third CONCACAF place in the final table. Honduras, level on points with an inferior goal difference, went into the play-offs. Gabriel Torres, with three historic goals, was Panama's leading marksman in qualifying.

GROUP G

TUNISIA

Tunisia are appearing in the finals for the fifth time, ambitious to progress beyond the first round. This was their sticking point in the finals on their debut in 1978 and then three times in succession between 1998 and 2006.

COACH

NABIL MAÂLOUL

Maâloul, 55, stepped in as manager for the decisive closing stages of the qualifying campaign in succession to Polish coach Henryk Kasperczak. He had appeared 74 times in midfield for Tunisia between 1985 and 1995 and played at the 1988 Olympic Games in Seoul. Maâloul played his club football with Espérance ST, CA Bizertin and Club Africain as well as Hannover 96 in Germany and Al-Ahli in Saudi Arabia. His coaching career includes national team experience as boss of Tunisia in 2013 and of Kuwait from 2014 until last year.

The *Eagles of Carthage* made history at the 1978 tournament by becoming the first African nation to win at the finals, when they defeated Mexico 3-1. That breakthrough helped persuade the world game to increase Africa's presence at the finals from one team to two in Spain in 1982.

Subsequent appearances saw Tunisia fall short in attack, managing only five goals in total in 1998, 2002 and 2006. However, they earned rich consolation by recording their only triumph in the Africa Cup of Nations. As hosts in 2004, they defeated Morocco 2-1 in the final.

The French first brought football to Tunis and a league was launched in 1921. Simultaneously, Tunisian clubs began competing in an annual North African Championship with sides from Algeria and Morocco. Racing Club (Tunis) won the inaugural event in 1919.

Racing were also the first domestic league champions. Espérance ST, destined to become one of the leading clubs not only in Tunisian but also African football, won their first league title in 1938.

An unofficial national team

HEADING FOR GLORY: Tunisia's Ghailan Chaalali (20, second right) celebrates with Youssef Msakni (7, second left) and other team-mates after striking what proved to be their winning goal in a 2-1 victory over DR Congo on 1 September last year.

ONES TO WATCH

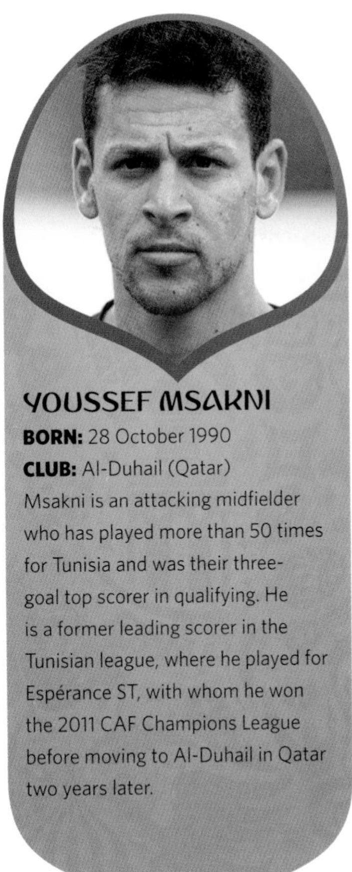

YOUSSEF MSAKNI

BORN: 28 October 1990

CLUB: Al-Duhail (Qatar)

Msakni is an attacking midfielder who has played more than 50 times for Tunisia and was their three-goal top scorer in qualifying. He is a former leading scorer in the Tunisian league, where he played for Espérance ST, with whom he won the 2011 CAF Champions League before moving to Al-Duhail in Qatar two years later.

BALBOULI

(Aymen Mathlouthi)

BORN: 14 September 1984

CLUB: Étoile du Sahel

Balbouli is considered Tunisia's finest goalkeeper and one of the best of all time in African football. He is captain of both the national team and his club, Étoile du Sahel, whom he joined in 2003 from Club Africain. Balbouli has played more than 79 times for Tunisia since making his debut in 2007.

RECORD AT PREVIOUS TOURNAMENTS

1930	did not exist
1934	did not exist
1938	did not exist
1950	did not exist
1954	did not exist
1958	did not enter
1962	did not qualify
1966	withdrew
1970	did not qualify
1974	did not qualify
1978	1st round
1982	did not qualify
1986	did not qualify
1990	did not qualify
1994	did not qualify
1998	1st round
2002	1st round
2006	1st round
2010	did not qualify
2014	did not qualify

competed against neighbours from Algeria, Oran, Constantine and Morocco in the 1930s and 1940s. National selections also played games against France B teams between 1928 and 1956, when Tunisia gained independence. The newly launched Tunisian FA joined both FIFA and CAF in 1960.

Tunisia subsequently became the first African nation after Egypt to appear at the Olympic Football Tournament. In 1962, they were the first French-speaking North African country to enter the Africa Cup of Nations, finishing third. Three years later, as hosts, they finished runners-up to Ghana.

The star player was captain and playmaker Abdelmajid Chetali, who was also coach of the team who made their FIFA World Cup finals debut in 1978. The next major era was in the mid-1990s, when Tunisia were Africa Cup of Nations runners-up and reached the finals of the 1998 FIFA World Cup under Polish coach Henryk Kasperczak. This was the first of their three successive appearances.

Kasperczak returned in 2015 to build a new team around stars such as goalkeeper-captain Balbouli, defenders Ali Maâloul and Syam Ben Youssef, midfielders Ferjani Sassi and Wahbi Khazri, and forwards Youssef Msakni and Fakhreddine Ben Youssef. A majority of the squad came from leading local clubs Espérance ST and Étoile du Sahel.

Tunisia began their quest for a place in Russia with a 4-2 aggregate victory over Mauritania in the second qualifying round. This propelled them into third round Group A, where Congo DR were their most difficult rivals. Tunisia were unbeaten yet led the table by a mere one point.

Decisive were last September's ties against Congo DR. Nabil Maâloul, who had succeeded Kasperczak as coach, masterminded a 2-1 home win and then a 2-2 draw in Kinshasa four days later. Tunisia were 2-0 down at one stage but recovered thanks to an own goal and then a priceless equaliser from Lyon-born Anice Badri.

A hat-trick from Youssef Msakni brought a 4-1 win in Guinea, which meant that a goalless draw at home to Libya on the last matchday was sufficient to take them to Russia.

GROUP G

ENGLAND

England head for Russia with fans hoping to see progress beyond the quarter-finals for only the second time since 1966. Their youngsters set a high standard with success in the FIFA U-17 and U-20 World Cups.

COACH

GARETH SOUTHGATE

Southgate, 47, took over the England job from Sam Allardyce one match into the FIFA World Cup qualifying campaign – and emerged with top marks. The former midfielder-cum-defender benefited from his wide experience of international football, having played 57 times for England between 1995 and 2004, including the finals of the 1996 UEFA European Championship and 1998 FIFA World Cup. At club level he played for Crystal Palace, Aston Villa and finally Middlesbrough, whom he also managed. Southgate then took on various roles with The Football Association, including the U-21 team manager.

The seniors have compiled an outstanding record in qualifying tournaments. When the *Three Lions* won their last 2018 group qualifier 2-1 in Lithuania, they had tallied 39 preliminary matches without defeat in both FIFA World Cup and UEFA European Championship qualifiers.

However, a stream of managers and players have discovered the complication of converting qualifying command into positive results at the finals.

The Football Association holds a historic place in the game as the first governing body, founded in 1863. England and Scotland played out the first official international match in November 1872 and The FA joined FIFA in 1906, two years after its formation.

Disagreements over matches against wartime opponents and then amateurism led to England's withdrawal from FIFA and their absence from the FIFA World Cup in the 1930s. They were joint favourites on their finals debut in Brazil in 1950 but failed to progress beyond the first round.

Quarter-final progress followed in 1954 and 1962 before England won

BETTER LATE THAN NEVER: England centre-forward Harry Kane scores the stoppage-time equaliser against Scotland to secure a 2-2 draw and keep his team's unbeaten European qualifying group run intact, in the match played at Hampden Park, Glasgow, on 10 June last year.

ONES TO WATCH

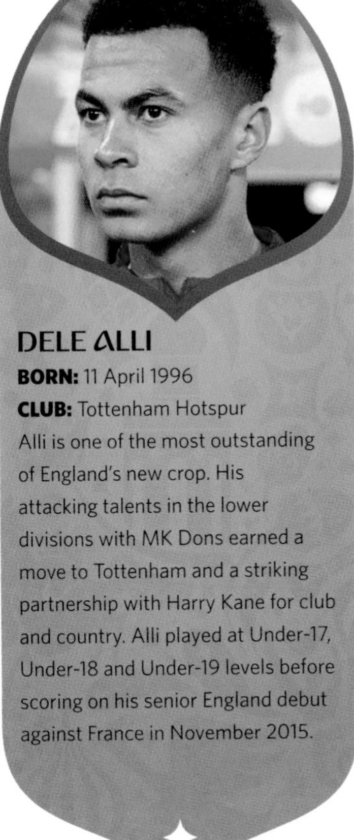

DELE ALLI

BORN: 11 April 1996

CLUB: Tottenham Hotspur

Alli is one of the most outstanding of England's new crop. His attacking talents in the lower divisions with MK Dons earned a move to Tottenham and a striking partnership with Harry Kane for club and country. Alli played at Under-17, Under-18 and Under-19 levels before scoring on his senior England debut against France in November 2015.

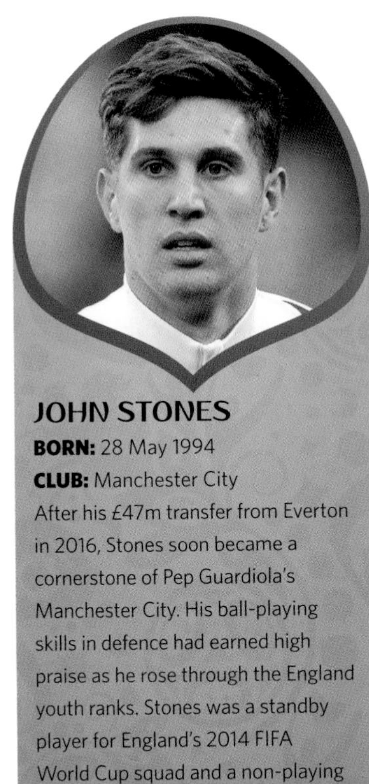

JOHN STONES

BORN: 28 May 1994

CLUB: Manchester City

After his £47m transfer from Everton in 2016, Stones soon became a cornerstone of Pep Guardiola's Manchester City. His ball-playing skills in defence had earned high praise as he rose through the England youth ranks. Stones was a standby player for England's 2014 FIFA World Cup squad and a non-playing member at UEFA EURO 2016.

RECORD AT PREVIOUS TOURNAMENTS

1930	did not enter
1934	did not enter
1938	did not enter
1950	1st round
1954	Quarter-finals
1958	1st round
1962	Quarter-finals
1966	CHAMPIONS
1970	Quarter-finals
1974	did not qualify
1978	did not qualify
1982	2nd round
1986	Quarter-finals
1990	4th place
1994	did not qualify
1998	2nd round
2002	Quarter-finals
2006	Quarter-finals
2010	2nd round
2014	1st round

the FIFA World Cup as hosts with a 4-2 extra-time victory over West Germany at Wembley in 1966. Geoff Hurst made history as the only man to score a hat-trick in the FIFA World Cup final, for an England team that included the legends Bobby Charlton and captain Bobby Moore.

Their FIFA World Cup defence ended at the quarter-finals stage in Mexico in 1970. England's best subsequent was the 1990 FIFA World Cup Italy, when they lost a semi-final on penalties to West Germany.

England have been present at the finals ever since 1998 under successive managers Glenn Hoddle, Sven-Göran Eriksson, Fabio Capello and Roy Hodgson, who left after UEFA EURO 2016 in France.

Sam Allardyce was briefly in charge – he had one game – before Gareth Southgate took over in September 2016. He made a winning start with a 2-0 defeat of Malta, thanks to goals from Daniel Sturridge and Dele Alli. A goalless draw in Slovenia was followed by a 3-0 home win over Scotland.

A goal in stoppage time from Tottenham centre-forward Harry Kane brought England a 2-2 draw away to the Scots at Hampden Park, Glasgow, in June 2017. Southgate's men then won their next three games to secure qualification for Russia with one match to spare. They finished eight points clear of second-placed Slovakia.

Kane was overall joint leading scorer in the group with five goals. Sturridge and Adam Lallana claimed two apiece.

Goalkeeper Joe Hart was the most experienced member of the squad that secured a place in the finals with more than 70 international appearances to his name. Chelsea's Gary Cahill was the only one of Hart's defensive colleagues who could boast more than 50 caps.

The qualifying campaign saw Liverpool's Jordan Henderson and Tottenham's Eric Dier develop a solid partnership in front of defence. In attack, the Tottenham partnership of Kane and Alli was supplemented by Lallana, Manchester City's Raheem Sterling and Manchester United's Marcus Rashford.

Southgate, on qualifying, cautioned that England were "still a work in progress". Now it is time to judge the pace of progress in Russia.

GROUP H

POLAND

Poland are back in the FIFA World Cup™ finals for the first time in 12 years. Twice previously they have reached the semi-finals, and this experienced outfit are led once again by record marksman Robert Lewandowski.

COACH

ADAM NAWALKA

Nawalka, 60, played 34 times in midfield for Poland between 1977 and 1980, including at the 1978 FIFA World Cup finals, before embarking on a coaching career. He was appointed national team coach in 2013 and was voted Coach of the Year in 2014 and 2015 on the way to steering Poland to the finals of the 2016 UEFA European Championship. His club appointments have included spells at Wisła Kraków, Zagłębie Lubin, Sandecja Nowy Sącz, Jagiellonia Białystok, GKS Katowice and Górnik Zabrze. He was also national team assistant to Leo Beenhakker in 2007.

Poland and the national team have existed for almost a century, independence in 1921 having been followed by a first international against Hungary. The Poles then made their debut at the FIFA World Cup finals in 1938, when Ernest Wilimowski scored a hat-trick in a dramatic first-round defeat by Brazil.

That was their last appearance at the pinnacle of the game for more than three decades.

A revival of Polish football was signalled by the progress of Górnik Zabrze to the UEFA European Cup Winners' Cup Final in 1969. Three years later, Poland won the football gold medal at the Summer Olympics in Munich with a side starring striker Włodzimierz Lubański, playmaker Kazimierz Deyna and left-winger Robert Gadocha.

For the 1974 FIFA World Cup, this trio were joined by striker Gregorz Lato and goalkeeper Jan Tomaszewski. Lato was the competition's leading scorer with seven goals as Poland finished third, defeating outgoing champions Brazil 1-0 for the honour. They reached the second round in 1978 and then, in 1982, placed third once more.

CHASING DOWN A RECORD: Poland captain Robert Lewandowski displays the hat-trick symbol after scoring his third goal in Poland's 6-1 victory away to Armenia in Yerevan last October which established him as his national team's all-time record marksman.

ONES TO WATCH

KAMIL GLIK

BORN: 3 February 1988
CLUB: Monaco (France)
Glik, a solid central defender, made his senior Poland debut in 2010 in the King's Cup in Thailand. He was not only the first player from Piast Gliwice to play for the national team but also marked the occasion with a goal. At the 2016 UEFA European Championship, in France, he converted penalty kicks in the decisive shoot-outs against both Switzerland and Portugal.

ARKADIUSZ MILIK

BORN: 28 February 1994
CLUB: Napoli (Italy)
Milik became one of Poland's most expensive players when the striker cost Napoli €35m in 2016. Previously, he had played for Górnik Zabrze, Bayer Leverkusen, FC Augsburg and Ajax. Hat-tricks at U-21 level earned Milik his senior debut and he scored consistently on Poland's runs in UEFA EURO 2016 and FIFA World Cup qualifiers.

RECORD AT PREVIOUS TOURNAMENTS

1930	did not enter
1934	did not enter
1938	1st round
1950	did not enter
1954	did not enter
1958	did not qualify
1962	did not qualify
1966	did not qualify
1970	did not qualify
1974	3rd place
1978	2nd round
1982	3rd place
1986	Round of 16
1990	did not qualify
1994	did not qualify
1998	did not qualify
2002	1st round
2006	1st round
2010	did not qualify
2014	did not qualify

A team led by a new attacking star in Zbigniew Boniek defeated France 3-2 in the play-off.

The political upheaval of the late 1980s brought major changes and challenges for the domestic game. These were reflected in the national team being unable to progress beyond the first-round groups at the FIFA World Cups of 2002 and 2006 and even at UEFA EURO 2012, when they had the advantage of co-hosting with Ukraine.

Then, despite the outstanding marksmanship of Germany-based centre-forward Robert Lewandowski, Poland were also absent from the FIFA World Cup finals in South Africa in 2010 and Brazil in 2014.

They regained a place among the elite, under coach Adam Nawalka, at the UEFA European Championship in 2016. Poland fell only in a quarter-final penalty shoot-out against eventual champions Portugal.

The backbone of that team has maintained their momentum to bring Poland to Russia – experienced players such as defenders Łukasz Pisczcek and Kamil Glik, midfielders Jakub Błazczykowski, Kamil Grosicki and Grzegorz Krychowiak, and forwards Arkadiusz Milik and captain Lewandowski.

The qualifying draw for Russia 2018 was kind to the Poles. None of their opponents in Group E had competed in either the recent European finals or at the 2014 FIFA World Cup in Brazil.

They began with a 2-2 draw in Kazakhstan and followed up with a 3-2 victory over Denmark powered by a Lewandowski hat-trick. He struck again with a stoppage-time penalty in the next 2-1 win over Armenia, and further victories over Romania and Montenegro saw them already leading the table by a clear six points at the halfway point in the qualifying schedule.

Lewandowski struck a second hat-trick in a 3-1 win over Romania. Their only setback was a 4-0 defeat in Denmark before Lewandowski led the recovery with yet another treble in a 6-1 win over Armenia. Poland finished five points clear of Denmark. The outstanding Lewandowski ended up with a European qualifying record 16 goals to become Poland's 51-goal all-time leading marksman.

GROUP H

SENEGAL

Senegal hope to make as outstanding an impression on the FIFA World Cup™ as they did in 2002. Back then, a team led by Aliou Cissé marked their debut on the game's greatest stage by reaching the quarter-finals.

COACH

ALIOU CISSÉ

Cissé, 42, took over in 2015 and guided Senegal to the quarter-finals of the Africa Cup of Nations last year. He already possessed FIFA World Cup pedigree as the defensive midfielder who captained his team to the quarter-finals in 2002 on their debut in the tournament. Previously Cissé held an appointment as interim manager in 2012 and then coach of the Olympic team. Cissé's playing career took him to French clubs Lille, Sedan, Paris Saint-Germain, Montpellier and Nîmes plus English outfits Birmingham City and Portsmouth.

The fact that the *Lions of Teranga* have appeared only once at the finals undervalues the talent and quality of their players down the years.

Senegal were one of the first newly independent countries from former French West Africa to qualify for the finals of the Cup of Nations in 1965. They finished fourth, were fourth again in 1990, quarter-finalists as hosts in 1992 and runners-up in 2002. In the final in Bamako, the capital of Mali, they lost 3-2 on penalties to Cameroon after a goalless draw.

That same team then progressed to the FIFA World Cup finals for the first time. Stars such as winger El Hadji Diouf and goalkeeper Tony Sulva not only shared the honour of competing in the opening match but made it memorable by defeating champions France 1-0 in Seoul. Pape "Papa" Bouba Diop scored the most famous goal in Senegalese history.

They proved this was no fluke by drawing 1-1 and 3-3 with Denmark and Uruguay, respectively, to reach the round of 16. There they beat Sweden 2-1 but lost 1-0 to an extra-time golden goal by Turkey in Osaka.

OFF TO A WINNING START: Moussa Sow (centre) and his team-mates react with delight to his goal which brought Senegal the security of a 2-0 lead at home to Cape Verde in Dakar in the opening game of Group D in the final round of the African qualifying competition.

ONES TO WATCH

SADIO MANÉ

BORN: 10 April 1992

CLUB: Liverpool (England)

Mané has been hailed as one of the most dangerous raiders in international football since his £34m transfer from Southampton to Liverpool two years ago. The winger has played 50 times for Senegal since making his debut in 2012. He then built his reputation with French club Metz and in Austrian football with Red Bull Salzburg.

CHEIKHOU KOUYATÉ

BORN: 21 December 1989

CLUB: West Ham United (England)

His midfield enforcer style means that Kouyaté, Senegal's captain, has been compared to France's former anchor Patrick Vieira. He made his senior national team debut in 2012 after starring at youth and Olympic level. Kouyaté's club career took him from Belgium's Anderlecht in 2014 to English Premier League outfit West Ham.

RECORD AT PREVIOUS TOURNAMENTS

1930	did not exist
1934	did not exist
1938	did not exist
1950	did not exist
1954	did not exist
1958	did not exist
1962	did not enter
1966	withdrew
1970	did not qualify
1974	did not qualify
1978	did not qualify
1982	did not qualify
1986	did not qualify
1990	did not qualify
1994	did not qualify
1998	did not qualify
2002	Quarter-finals
2006	did not qualify
2010	did not qualify
2014	did not qualify

Momentum has been maintained at continental level with mostly continuing participation in the finals of the Africa Cup of Nations. But a return to the FIFA World Cup has eluded them until now.

In the qualifying tournament, Senegal opened up in the second round with a 5-2 aggregate win over Madagascar. Captain Cheikhou Kouyaté, Pape Moussa Konaté and Mame Biram Diouf secured a decisive 3-0 victory in the second leg in front of their own fans in Dakar.

Senegal's third-round group was confused by events in an early game against South Africa. The *Lions of Teranga* had opened with a 2-0 win over Cape Verde, but the result of their next outing, a 2-1 defeat in South Africa, was later annulled by FIFA following the suspension of the Ghanaian match referee Joseph Lamptey.

Subsequently, Senegal secured draws home and away with Burkina Faso, an away win over Cape Verde and a further 2-0 victory in the replayed match away to South Africa. Diafra Sakho and Cheikh N'Doye scored the late goals that assured coach Aliou Cissé's men of qualification for the finals in Russia with one match to play.

Cissé's players are anything but inexperienced. Defence is built around Lamine Gassama, Kalidou Koulibaly, Kara Mbodj and Salif Sané who play their club football in Turkey, Italy, Belgium and Germany with Alanyaspor, Napoli, Anderlecht and Hannover respectively. Similarly, captain Kouyaté and fellow midfielder Idrissa Gana Gueye are established in the English Premier League with West Ham United and Everton.

Liverpool's Sadio Mané carries Senegal's attacking hopes in partnership with Moussa Sow from Shabab Al-Ahli in the UAE. But, above all, they can draw on the FIFA World Cup experience of coach Cissé. As captain in 2002, he knows exactly what can be achieved.

The coach's experience of national team pressures and the personal inspiration he can provide after his own leadership achievements in 2002 have been acknowledged openly by his players all along the road to Russia.

GROUP H

COLOMBIA

Coach José Pékerman and his Colombian *Cafeteros* had to wait until the last matchday of the South American qualifying competition before being free to celebrate their return to the FIFA World Cup™ finals.

COACH

JOSÉ PÉKERMAN

Pékerman, 68, is one of Argentina's outstanding coaching exports. He played for Argentinos Juniors and Colombia's Independiente Medellín before injury ended his career at 28. He worked in youth football in Chile and Colombia before being appointed as senior youth coach by Argentina, with whom he won three FIFA U-20 World Cups. In 2004, he became senior national coach and led Argentina to the quarter-finals of the FIFA World Cup in 2006. In 2012, after a spell in Mexico, he was appointed coach of Colombia, whom he also led to the FIFA World Cup quarter-finals in 2014.

A 1-1 draw in Peru, courtesy of a goal from star midfielder James Rodríguez, secured their ticket to the finals. Fourth place in the South American qualifying mini-league delighted not only their own fans but also supporters all around the world who had been entertained by Colombia's FIFA World Cup adventures down the years.

The Colombian FA was founded in 1924 and joined FIFA in 1936. Turbulence within Colombian society and the country's football kept the national team on the international sidelines throughout the 1950s. Hence their first appearance at the FIFA World Cup finals was in Chile in 1962, when they marked their debut campaign with a dramatic 4-4 draw against the Soviet Union.

Colombia were then absent from the finals for a further 28 years before a fine team, coached by Francisco Maturana, returned to the game's greatest stage in Italy in 1990. A side featuring goalkeeper René Orlando Higuita, defender Andrés Escobar and bouffant-haired playmaker Carlos Valderrama reached the round of 16 before

THE MAN IN FORM: James Rodriguez, one of Colombia's heroes from their FIFA World Cup campaign in Brazil in 2014, extends his reputation by scoring the goal which earned his country a 1-0 win at home to Bolivia in Barranquilla in March last year.

ONES TO WATCH

DAVID OSPINA

BORN: 31 August 1988
CLUB: Arsenal (England)
Ospina has been the first-choice goalkeeper for Colombia (when fit) ever since the 2010 FIFA World Cup qualifiers, and he now has than 80 caps to his name. He was a key member of the team that reached the FIFA World Cup quarter-finals in 2014 and finished third at the *Copa América* in 2016. Club successes have included being Arsenal's FA Cup-winning goalkeeper in 2017.

RADAMEL FALCAO

BORN: 10 February 1986
CLUB: AS Monaco (France)
Falcao is Colombia's all-time record marksman with around 30 goals to his name in more than 70 internationals. He made his name with River Plate in Argentina in a free-scoring club career that has included UEFA Europa League successes with Porto and Atlético Madrid. A serious knee injury forced him to miss the 2014 FIFA World Cup.

RECORD AT PREVIOUS TOURNAMENTS

1930	did not enter
1934	did not enter
1938	withdrew
1950	did not enter
1954	suspended
1958	did not qualify
1962	1st round
1966	did not qualify
1970	did not qualify
1974	did not qualify
1978	did not qualify
1982	did not qualify
1986	did not qualify
1990	Round of 16
1994	1st round
1998	1st round
2002	did not qualify
2006	did not qualify
2010	did not qualify
2014	Quarter-finals

losing 2-1 in extra time to Cameroon.

The 1994 FIFA World Cup qualifying competition saw Colombia record a dramatic 5-0 win over Argentina in Buenos Aires, but they failed to fulfil their potential in the United States. Tragically, after the team was eliminated in the first round and returned home, Escobar was murdered.

Colombia were back in the finals in France in 1998 but were eliminated in the first round after a concluding group defeat by England. They did not return to the finals until 2014, when they achieved their finest performance thus far by reaching the quarter-finals, where they lost 2-1 to their Brazilian hosts.

Russia 2018 will see Colombia's sixth appearance in the finals. They will benefit not only from the previous FIFA World Cup wisdom of coach Pékerman but from the international experience of a nucleus of players with more than 50 appearances each for their country.

These include goalkeeper David Ospina from England's Arsenal, defender Cristián Zapata from Italy's Milan plus midfielders Carlos Sánchez and Juan Cuadrado from Italian outfits Fiorentina and Juventus, respectively, as well as Rodríguez, who has been on loan at Germany's Bayern Munich from Spain's Real Madrid. The attack is led by national team captain and record marksman Radamel Falcao of 2017 French league champions Monaco.

Colombia made an ideal start to the South American qualifying campaign by defeating Peru 2-0 at home in Barranquilla with goals from Teófilo Gutiérrez and Edwin Cardona but they suffered an immediate setback with a 3-0 defeat in Uruguay.

In March 2016, they regained winning momentum when a stoppage-time goal from Cardona brought a 3-2 win in Bolivia. Successive victories over Ecuador and Venezuela saw Pékerman's men back on track. Finally, a 1-1 draw away to Peru in Lima saw them qualify for the finals. That one point proved crucial – it was their margin of advantage in the table ahead of the fifth-placed Peruvians.

James Rodríguez was Colombia's leading marksman in qualifying with six goals, followed by three-goal Cardona and Falcao with two.

GROUP H

JAPAN

Japan have been ever-present at the finals of the past five FIFA World Cup™ tournaments but have yet to progress beyond the round of 16. Taking that next step forward will be the focus of coach Vahid Halilhodžić.

COACH

VAHID HALILHODŽIĆ

Halilhodžić, 65, played 15 times in attack for the former Yugoslavia between 1976 and 1985 while starring for Velež Mostar and then Nantes and Paris Saint-Germain in France. His coaching career took in Morocco, France, Turkey, Saudi Arabia, Côte d'Ivoire and Croatia before he guided Algeria past the first round of the FIFA World Cup for the first time in their history in 2014. Halilhožić returned to Trabzonspor in Turkey for a second time before being appointed Japan coach in succession to Mexican Javier Aguirre in 2015.

The *Blue Samurai* had signalled their arrival among the powers of the Asian game with the manner of their co-hosting, alongside Korea Republic, of the FIFA World Cup finals in 2002, the first staging in Asia. The organisation was excellent while the national team, finalists for the first time four years earlier in France, reached the second round before losing to Turkey.

With a sound professional foundation in the high-level J.League, the national team went on from strength to strength. Stars such as Hidetoshi Nakata and Junichi Inamoto shone, although Japan fell in the first round of the 2006 FIFA World Cup in Germany.

A further demonstration of the country's increasing power was that, with a recast team in 2010 in South Africa, they reached the second round on foreign soil for the first time. A team with outstanding new players such as Keisuke Honda and goalkeeper Eiji Kawashima fell only in a penalty shoot-out after a goalless extra-time draw with Paraguay.

Kawashima remains one of the stars of the current squad

WINNING REASON TO BELIEVE: Yosuke Ideguchi (2) celebrates after scoring Japan's second goal to clinch a 2-0 victory over Australia in Saitama on 31 August last year, a result which secured his country's place in the finals for the sixth time in succession.

ONES TO WATCH

SHINJI KAGAWA

BORN: 17 March 1989
CLUB: Borussia Dortmund (Germany)

Kagawa has built his international reputation from almost a decade playing in top-flight European football with Borussia Dortmund, Manchester United and now Dortmund again. The hard-working midfielder has played around 90 times for Japan and was voted AFC Asian Footballer of the Year in 2012.

KEISUKE HONDA

BORN: 13 June 1986
CLUB: CF Pachuca (Mexico)

Honda, an attacking midfielder, has played more than 90 times for Japan since making his debut in 2008. He was a member of Japan's squad at the FIFA World Cup finals both in 2010 in South Africa and in 2014 in Brazil. He was voted the tournament's best player when Japan defeated Australia in Doha in 2011 to win the AFC Asian Cup.

RECORD AT PREVIOUS TOURNAMENTS

1930	did not enter
1934	did not enter
1938	withdrew
1950	withdrew
1954	did not qualify
1958	did not enter
1962	did not qualify
1966	did not enter
1970	did not qualify
1974	did not qualify
1978	did not qualify
1982	did not qualify
1986	did not qualify
1990	did not qualify
1994	did not qualify
1998	1st round
2002	Round of 16
2006	1st round
2010	Round of 16
2014	1st round

along with senior defenders Yuto Nagatomo and Maya Yoshida, midfielders Shinji Kagawa, Keisuke Honda and captain Makoto Hasebe, plus Leicester City's Shinji Okazaki and Germany-based Genki Haraguchi and Takashi Inui in attack.

Football had always taken a back seat in Japan's sporting hierarchy until the Japanese FA decided, in the early 1990s, to launch its ambitious bid to be the first Asian hosts of the FIFA World Cup. That campaign included the 1993 launch of the J.League, with new clubs backed by private sponsors and local authorities.

Foreign stars such as Zico of Brazil, Gary Lineker of England, Italy's Toto Schillaci and Pierre Littbarski of Germany were signed to help promote the league at home and abroad, and the success of that long-term strategy continues to be evident. Japan have won the AFC Asian Cup four times and the youth teams have impressed consistently in both men's and women's competitions.

Japan were seeded to the second round of the Asian section for their latest FIFA World Cup qualifying challenge. They won seven and drew one of their matches, scoring a remarkable 27 goals and conceding none. The only points they dropped were in a goalless home draw against Singapore, and their most decisive victory was a 6-0 win over Afghanistan in Tehran. Kagawa and Okazaki scored two goals apiece.

Coach Halilhodžić and his men faced a challenging task in the third round, in a Group B that included former FIFA World Cup finalists in Australia, Iraq, Saudi Arabia and United Arab Emirates. In the end, they secured their place in the finals in Russia on the penultimate matchday when goals from Takuma Asano and Yosuke Ideguchi provided a 2-0 victory over Australia in front of a 59,000 crowd in the Saitama Stadium.

The Japanese were thus uncatchable at the top of the table despite a 1-0 defeat in Saudi Arabia by the group runners-up in the last game. Honda and Kagawa were Japan's leading individual marksmen in the overall qualifying competition, with seven and six goals apiece.

adidas
10

2018 FIFA World Cup™ Superstars

The FIFA World Cup™ offers the greatest stage for the greatest players. Portugal's Cristiano Ronaldo and Argentina's Lionel Messi, multiple award-winners at national team, club and individual levels, expect to lead the parade of superstars in Russia. But every country has its heroes. A highly talented mix of personalities in goal, defence, midfield and attack carry the hopes and dreams of hosts Russia and the other 31 competing nations.

LEFT: Argentina's Lionel Messi embraces the moment after scoring the winning goal against Chile in their FIFA World Cup qualifier in the Estadio Monumental in Buenos Aires on 23 March 2017.

STAR PLAYER

TIM CAHILL

Tim Cahill, with a goal every two games, has been Australia's most outstanding performer in the history of the FIFA World Cup™, having made his finals debut back in Germany in 2006.

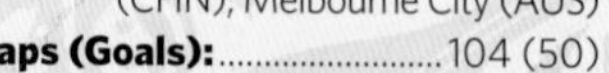

FACTS AND FIGURES

Born: 6 December 1979
Position: Midfield
Clubs: Millwall (ENG), Everton (ENG), New York Red Bulls (USA), Shanghai Shenhua (CHN), Hangzhou Greentown (CHN), Melbourne City (AUS)
Caps (Goals): 104 (50)

The goalscoring midfielder has topped a century of national team appearances since his debut in a friendly against South Africa in London back in 2004. He is also the first Australian to have scored at a FIFA World Cup and, after his exploits in 2006, 2010 and 2014, he is their top scorer with five goals.

Born in Sydney, Cahill lived in Samoa for three years as a child and, at 14, played for the Samoans in the 1994 Oceania U-20 Championship. That international registration forced him to turn down FIFA World Cup selection for the Republic of Ireland in 2002.

Cahill had Irish grandparents and had made an impression in English football with Millwall, whose manager, Mick McCarthy, then took up the Irish job. Bad news for the Irish was good news for Australia. Two years later, FIFA eased youth eligibility regulations and Cahill chose to play for the land of his birth.

His impact was immediate. He helped Australia progress to the quarter-finals at the Olympic Games in Athens in 2004 and then, in 2006, to reach the FIFA World Cup finals for the first time in 30 years.

Cahill scored twice in the *Socceroos*' opening win over Japan, and they went on to the round of 16 before falling to eventual champions Italy. His next finals were less rewarding, however. Cahill was sent off in Australia's first game against Germany in 2010 and the team went home early despite his goal in a subsequent game against Serbia.

By 2014, Cahill had developed into his nation's all-time leading marksman: attending the finals for a third time in Brazil, he scored a magnificent goal against the Netherlands. More crucial goals followed on the qualifying road to Russia. None, however, may have been more important than the extra-time winner in the Asian play-off second leg against Syria.

Playing at a fourth FIFA World Cup would be yet another mark of distinction for the *Socceroos*' record man.

"Timmy is the greatest ever. He's just a freak. He's just got real belief in himself, a real unique and extraordinary individual. It's amazing how he keeps pushing himself."
Ange Postecoglou, former Australia manager

STAR PLAYER

KEVIN DE BRUYNE

Kevin De Bruyne has established himself as a leader, in midfield, of the new generation of Belgian stars who have reclaimed the historic international pride of the *Red Devils*.

De Bruyne's displays in the FIFA World Cup qualifying competition for Russia and with Manchester City in the English Premier League have established him as one of the most impressive figures in the European game, both powerful and creative.

The career of a future world football superstar began with KVE Drongen, based in his home town in central Belgium. He quickly progressed up the ladder with KAA Gent and KRC Genk, with whom he became a domestic champion. Then it was on to Chelsea, a loan spell with Werder Bremen and a €30m move to VfL Wolfsburg.

Here De Bruyne's displays for both club and country earned a return to the English Premier League with Manchester City. Since 2015, and over the past two seasons under Pep Guardiola, De Bruyne's career has gone from strength to strength. This has suited Belgium perfectly.

De Bruyne played for Belgium at U-18, U-19 and U-21 levels before making his senior *Red Devils'* debut in August 2010 away to Finland. His first goal for his country followed two months later away to Serbia. Subsequently, De Bruyne established himself in the starting line-up ahead of the 2014 FIFA World Cup finals. In Brazil, De Bruyne featured in wins over Algeria and Russia, then starred in the round-of-16 victory over the United States. He opened the scoring in extra time and set up Romelu Lukaku for what proved to be the decisive goal in a 2-1 win.

De Bruyne's journey ended in the next round against Argentina, but the experience proved important as he progressed to lead Belgium to the quarter-finals again at the UEFA European Championship in 2016.

His value has been underlined by more than 50 international appearances in six years as well as the £55m fee paid by Manchester City in 2015. That was then a record for a Belgian footballer, a status that his skill has justified ever since.

FACTS AND FIGURES

Born: 28 June 1991
Position: Midfield
Clubs: KRC Genk (BEL), Chelsea (ENG), Werder Bremen (GER), VfL Wolfsburg (GER), Manchester City (ENG)
Caps (Goals): 58 (13)

"He can do absolutely everything but he's also the most humble, the most shy guy. You don't find many players like this. He is one of the best players I've ever seen in my life."
Pep Guardiola, Manchester City manager

STAR PLAYER

CHRISTIAN ERIKSEN

Christian Eriksen justified his three consecutive awards as Danish Footballer of the Year with the hat-trick against the Republic of Ireland which lifted Denmark back into the FIFA World Cup™ finals.

The 26-year-old's goals inspired a 5-1 win over the Republic of Ireland, which clinched victory by the same score in the European play-offs. Hence Eriksen's burgeoning talents will be on display at the pinnacle of the world game for the second time.

Eriksen began with Odense Boldklub, transferred to Ajax Amsterdam in 2008 and then, in 2013, to Tottenham Hotspur, where he has become a fans' favourite, starring in both the English Premier League and the Champions League.

Unlike many of his current Danish team-mates, Eriksen has already experienced the drama of the FIFA World Cup. In 2010, at 18, he was the youngest player at the finals in South Africa. Eriksen was a late substitute in defeats by the Netherlands and Japan, which ended the Danish campaign in the first round.

However, his evident talent secured him the Danish Footballer Player of the Year award and, thanks to his move to Ajax, the Dutch Football Talent of the Year. He transferred to Tottenham in 2013 after winning the Dutch league title.

Eriksen took his first steps up the national team ladder with the Danish youth team and made his senior debut in a pre-FIFA World Cup friendly against Austria in March 2010. At the time, manager Morten Olsen refuted concerns about Eriksen's lack of experience by hailing his "huge potential", praise since vindicated.

Soon after the return from South Africa, Eriksen became a regular in the Danish starting line-up and scored his first international goal in a UEFA European Championship tie against Iceland in June 2011.

He started all of Denmark's three matches in the first round at UEFA EURO 2012, but the national team then failed to reach the finals of the FIFA World Cup in 2014 and UEFA EURO 2016. Hence the significance of his match-winning hat-trick against the Republic of Ireland; play-off success ended Denmark's six-year absence from the main international stage.

FACTS AND FIGURES

Born: 14 February 1992
Position: Midfield
Clubs: Ajax (NED), Tottenham Hotspur (ENG)
Caps (Goals): 75 (21)

"He is always very aggressive in possession and always working very hard to improve. It's important for any team to have the number of goals he scores, coming from midfield."
Mauricio Pochettino, Tottenham Hotspur manager

STAR PLAYER

JAVIER "Chicharito" HERNÁNDEZ

Javier "Chicharito" Hernández brings family pedigree to the 2018 FIFA World Cup Russia™. His father, also Javier, was a member of *El Tri's* squad in 1986 and grandfather Tomás Balcázar played in 1954.

Destiny was clearly calling and the teenage "Little Pea" launched upon a professional career that has seen him established as Mexico's all-time leading scorer. The pinnacle of achievement thus far was in the 2011 CONCACAF Gold Cup, when Mexico's victory owed an enormous debt to the seven goals that also helped win him the best player and top marksman awards.

Hernández's debut at a world championship was at the FIFA U-20 World Cup in Canada in 2007 and he made his first senior appearance two years later, providing the assist for Mexico's consolation goal in a 2-1 defeat by Colombia.

Next time out, in 2010, he scored his first two goals for *El Tri* in a 5-0 win over Bolivia. Now, eight years later, he has outstripped the national team's scoring records once held by former FIFA World Cup leaders such as Jared Borgetti (46) and Cuauhtémoc Blanco (39).

The FIFA World Cup in South Africa in 2010 saw Hernández emulate his father and grandfather by achieving selection for the finals. Not only that, but he scored a goal in a 2-0 win over France, just as grandfather Tomás Balcázar had managed in the 1954 finals in Switzerland. A first hat-trick followed the next year in a 5-0 win over El Salvador in the Mexicans' triumphant 2011 CONCACAF Gold Cup campaign.

At the 2014 FIFA World Cup Brazil, Hernández and Mexico reached the round of 16, but he missed a further Gold Cup success the next year after breaking a collarbone in a pre-tournament friendly against Honduras.

Simultaneously, his club career was going from strength to strength. He started out with home city club CD Guadalajara and moved to Europe, and England, with Manchester United in 2010. In 2014, he was loaned to Real Madrid for a year and then widened his experience with two seasons in the German *Bundesliga* at Bayer Leverkusen. Last year saw him return to the English Premier League with West Ham United.

FACTS AND FIGURES

Born: 1 June 1988
Position: Forward
Clubs: CD Guadalajara (MEX), Manchester United (ENG), Real Madrid (ESP), Bayer Leverkusen (GER), West Ham United (ENG)
Caps (Goals): 99 (49)

"What Chicharito is achieving right now will go down in history. His movement in the area is great because he is so quick to take advantage of space and lose his markers."
Luiz Hernández, former Mexico international

STAR PLAYER

ANDRÉS INIESTA

Andrés Iniesta heads for the FIFA World Cup™ aiming to write another page in Spanish history, just as he did when scoring the winning goal against the Netherlands in the 2010 final in South Africa.

FACTS AND FIGURES

Born: .... 11 May 1984
Position: .... Midfield
Clubs: .... FC Barcelona (ESP)
Caps (Goals): 123 (13)

The FC Barcelona club captain has won more than 30 trophies with country and club, and remains, even in his thirties, one of the most mobile and astute playmakers in the international game.

Iniesta was marked out for superstardom at an early age. He played almost 50 times for Spain at all youth levels and was a champion at European U-16 level in 2001 and U-19 in 2002. In 2003, Iniesta was captain of the Spanish team that finished runners-up to Brazil in the FIFA World Youth Championship in Abu Dhabi.

Veteran coach Luis Aragonés promptly called him up to *La Roja*'s senior squad in the run-up to the FIFA World Cup finals in Germany in 2006. Iniesta made his debut in a May friendly against Russia in Albacete where, as a youngster, he had first impressed Barcelona. In the finals, he played only in a first-round victory over Saudi Arabia before Spain's campaign ended against France in the round of 16.

That was the last time Spain – with Iniesta playing a key role in their possession game – failed to win a major tournament until 2014. Over the next eight years, Iniesta was a member of the Barcelona nucleus that excelled. With playmaking partner Xavi Hernández in particular, he helped Spain win the 2008 and 2012 UEFA European Championships as well as the 2010 FIFA World Cup. That was where Iniesta scored the extra-time winning goal against the Dutch in Soccer City, Johannesburg.

Iniesta was still present, tirelessly linking defence with attack, when Spain lost their grips on first the FIFA World Cup trophy in Brazil four years ago and then the European crown in France in 2016. But neither of these setbacks had any impact on the magnificent reputation Iniesta has developed thanks to the remarkable consistency he has shown down the years at international level.

Simultaneously, Iniesta has been burnishing his reputation with his achievements for Barcelona: the team has won eight league titles, 11 domestic cups and Super Cups, and a further nine world and European club prizes.

"I saw him up close playing with him and saw how he can change a game playing against him. He is always driving his team forward and his record of trophies and titles is amazing."
Thierry Henry, former France striker

STAR PLAYER

HARRY KANE

Harry Kane's restless attacking style, allied to lethal marksmanship, has marked him out as the modern inheritor of the traditions of great England strikers.

The Tottenham captain has taken his place in a line that stretches down from the likes of the prolific Tommy Lawton, Jimmy Greaves, Geoff Hurst, Gary Lineker and Alan Shearer.

Kane is no overnight shooting star. He has put in the essential hard work to build a career of such significance for both country and club. He made his first-team debut for Tottenham in an August 2011 UEFA Europa League match against Hearts. But before establishing himself at Tottenham he was loaned out to "learn his trade" in the lower divisions at Leyton Orient, Millwall and Leicester City and at Norwich City in the Premier League.

In 2014-15, Kane exploded at the top level, scoring 31 goals in all competitions, including 21 in the league, to earn the Young Player of the Year from the Professional Footballers' Association. He was league top scorer in both 2015-16 and 2016-17 and already has netted more than 100 goals for Tottenham.

Similarly, at international level, Kane has steadily worked his way up the England ladder, representing his country at U-17, U-19, U-20 and U-21 levels. He played and scored at the FIFA U-20 World Cup and was a regular with the U-21s when he made his senior debut against Lithuania as a second-half substitute in a UEFA EURO 2016 qualifying match, needing only 90 seconds to open his account from Raheem Sterling's cross. Kane's first start for England came a few days later in a 1-1 draw with Italy in Turin.

From that point on, Kane has been a first-choice starter for England when fit. Not only that but he was appointed England captain for the first time for the 2-2 FIFA World Cup qualifying draw against Scotland at Hampden Park, Glasgow. Last October he scored the stoppage-time goal that defeated Lithuania, enabling England to secure their place in the 2018 FIFA World Cup Russia.

England manager Gareth Southgate has no doubt about Kane's quality. He said: "His finishing quality is as good as anyone I've played with or worked with. I'm never in doubt that, any time he has a good opportunity, it'll be on target and there's a fair chance he scores. We're fortunate to have him."

"You could see from the start that Harry was deadly. The quality of finishing in training took me back to watching Alan Shearer and Robbie Fowler."
Gareth Southgate, England manager

FACTS AND FIGURES

Born: 28 July 1993
Position: Centre-forward
Clubs: Tottenham Hotspur (ENG).
Loans: Leyton Orient, Millwall, Norwich City, Leicester City
Caps (Goals): 23 (12)

STAR PLAYER

ROBERT LEWANDOWSKI

Robert Lewandowski's goal-scoring achievements at national team and club levels have established him as one of the most feared centre-forwards of the modern era.

Lewandowski lived up to that status in the qualifying tournament for the FIFA World Cup in Russia by scoring 16 goals - a European qualifying tournament record. This meant that the Poles headed their Group H by a decisive five points from Denmark.

Lewandowski's marksmanship has recalled Poland's finest FIFA World Cup era in the 1970s and early 1980s, and he even scored on his debut, aged 20, against San Marino in September 2008. In 2012, when Poland and Ukraine were co-hosts for the UEFA European Championship, he led their attack and scored the tournament's opening goal against Greece. His leadership qualities were acknowledged a year later when he was appointed national team captain.

Poland missed the 2014 FIFA World Cup finals in Brazil, but Lewandowski's goals soon returned in qualifiers for the UEFA European Championship in 2016, when he tied the tournament record with 13.

Poland's campaign ended in the quarter-finals, but that disappointment did not blunt the skipper's appetite for goals as his 16 in the qualifying competition to reach Russia showed. Only Mohammad Al-Sahlawi from Saudi Arabia and Ahmed Khalil from the United Arab Emirates matched his 16 goals, which included hat-tricks at home to Denmark and away to Armenia.

Lewandowski first made the Polish game sit up and take notice when, as an 18-year-old, he was leading marksman in the third division with Znicz Pruszków, helping them secure promotion to the second division, when he again became the leading marksman. A 2008 transfer to Lech Poznań saw him win the league, Polish Cup and Polish Super Cup, as well as another top-scorer prize, which secured a move to Germany with Borussia Dortmund in 2010.

Goals and glory followed to the tune of two league titles, one cup and a runners-up medal in the UEFA Champions League. A further move to Bayern resulted in more league and leading scorer prizes, and he ranks in the top 10 of all-time leading *Bundesliga* marksmen.

"Robert is a great and fantastic football player. It is impossible to compare him with anyone. He is like a postage stamp – his value will grow the longer time goes on."
Zbigniew Boniek, President of the Polish Football Association

FACTS AND FIGURES

Born: 21 August 1988
Position: Centre-forward
Clubs: Znicz Pruszków (POL), Lech Poznań (POL), Borussia Dortmund (GER), Bayern Munich (GER)
Caps (Goals): 91 (51)

STAR PLAYER

LIONEL MESSI

Lionel Messi's brilliance has left team-mates, opponents, coaches and fans all grasping for superlatives to extol a talent which has earned him a place among the all-time greats.

Argentina boast many of the greatest footballers in the game's history, from early FIFA World Cup heroes such as Luis Monti and Raimundo Orsi to Alfredo di Stéfano and Ángel Labruna and then on to FIFA World Cup-winners Mario Kempes and the incomparable Diego Maradona.

Messi's own place in the pantheon of the game reflects not only his skill on the ball as well as his selfless teamwork but also the sheer weight of statistics cementing his reputation.

The "Atomic Flea" has played all his football in Spain after having left Newell's Old Boys in Rosario at 13 to join Barcelona. There, at a club always replete with stars jostling for first-team favour, he rapidly rose up through the ranks.

Messi has won the FIFA top player prize on five occasions to burnish a club record that includes around 30 club titles at international and Spanish domestic levels plus 20 top-scorer awards and more than 100 individual prizes.

He has scored more than 600 goals in his career with records for most goals in *La Liga* (362), in one *La Liga* season (50), in an overall European season (73) and in a calendar year (91). Messi is also the record non-European marksman in the history of the UEFA Champions League.

The only arena in which Messi has a gap to fill is in senior competition for Argentina. He inspired Argentina's victory in the FIFA U-20 World Cup in 2005 and was an Olympic gold medal-winner in 2008. But Argentina, in the Messi era, have never won the *Copa América* or FIFA World Cup – yet.

Argentina's campaigns with Messi on board were halted in the quarter-finals by Germany in both 2006 and 2010. In 2014, Messi's Argentina lost to Germany yet again, this time to a single goal after extra time in the final. Messi's consolation was to be officially hailed as the best player in the finals. But he will return to the finals intending to go one better.

FACTS AND FIGURES

Born: .... 24 June 1987
Position: .... Forward
Clubs: .... FC Barcelona (ESP)
Caps (Goals): 123 (61)

"I have never seen a player of such quality and personality. Before a game you plan for everything, then Messi produces a move no one expects, to change the game in an instant."
Fabio Capello, former England and Russia manager

STAR PLAYER

JOHN OBI MIKEL

John Obi Mikel has been a stalwart leader for Nigeria at both the last FIFA World Cup™ and Olympic Games, bringing control and stability in midfield and defence for the *Super Eagles*.

The 31-year-old's club career has been rewarded with ten winners' medals from a decade in the English Premier League with Chelsea while his international record includes a bronze medal from the 2016 Summer Olympics.

Mikel is a product of the youth academy that developed Nigerian FIFA World Cup star Celestine Babayaro. His first call-up was for the 2003 FIFA U-17 World Championship in Finland. Two years later he won the silver ball as the tournament's second-best player at the FIFA World Youth Championship in the Netherlands. Nigeria reached the final, only to lose to an Argentina team inspired by Lionel Messi.

A few weeks later, Mikel was promoted to make his senior debut for the *Super Eagles* as a substitute in a 1-0 friendly win over Libya. Mikel's next full international game was in the 2006 Africa Cup of Nations. Against Zimbabwe, he made a dramatic impact as a substitute, first delivering the corner from which Nigeria went ahead, then scoring his first national team goal himself. Two years later, on the same Nations Cup stage, Mikel again provided a goal and an assist to help Nigeria into the quarter-finals, where they lost to hosts Ghana.

Mikel was unlucky to miss the 2010 FIFA World Cup in South Africa because of injury, but he was back at his most commanding when Nigeria won the 2013 Africa Cup of Nations. A year later, in Brazil, he made up for lost time in FIFA World Cup terms: he was voted man of the match in the opening 0-0 draw against IR Iran on Nigeria's route to the knockout stage for the first time since 1998.

Back in Brazil, two years later, Mikel was a bronze-medal winner at the Summer Olympics just as his club career was about to take a new turn with a move to China's Tianjin TEDA.

Mikel had started in Europe with Lyn, in Oslo, before a decade with Chelsea saw him enjoy success in the UEFA Champions League and UEFA Europa League, as well as winning two Premier League titles, four FA Cups and two League Cups.

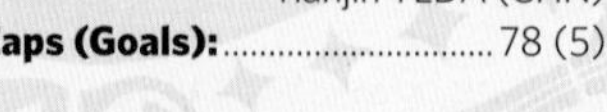

FACTS AND FIGURES

Born: 22 April 1987
Position: Midfield
Clubs: Lyn (NOR), Chelsea (ENG), Tianjin TEDA (CHN)
Caps (Goals): 78 (5)

"Mikel is the ideal player to bring balance to any team he plays in. He knows the game very well and how to cope with everything. To see such a player defend so elegantly is a beautiful thing."
Guus Hiddink, former Netherlands and Korea Republic coach

STAR PLAYER

KEYLOR NAVAS

Keylor Navas proved himself no mere shooting star after he followed up his brilliant campaign in goal for Costa Rica at the 2014 FIFA World Cup™ by winning the UEFA Champions League with Real Madrid.

Navas was a hero back home in Central America before his courage, sure handling and reflexes turned him into an international sensation in Brazil.

The goalkeeper from Saprissa made his senior debut in 2008 in a FIFA World Cup qualifying tie against Suriname. Although only 22, he kept his place for the CONCACAF Gold Cup the following year when he was named as the tournament's best goalkeeper.

Costa Rica failed to make it to the FIFA World Cup finals in 2010 but progressed to Brazil in 2014. Navas was outstanding, conceding only one goal, to Uruguay, in the group stage and keeping clean sheets against both Italy and England. Navas conceded only one further goal in the 1-1 draw with Greece in the round of 16 and then dived full length to magnificently save the crucial spotkick from Theofanis Gekas.

Navas was voted man of the match three times and was among the nominees for the Golden Glove award. Ultimately he was beaten, but only by Germany's FIFA World Cup-winner Manuel Neuer.

By this time Navas had long been playing his club football in Spain. He left Saprissa in 2010, after six league championship victories and one CONCACAF Champions League Cup, to join Albacete in the Spanish second division. A transfer to Levante and a starring role in the top division saw Navas hailed as *La Liga*'s top goalkeeper in the 2013-14 season.

His continuing brilliance at the FIFA World Cup saw Navas signed by Real Madrid as a successor to the great Iker Casillas. Immediately he was an international winner in the UEFA Super Cup and the FIFA Club World Cup.

More success followed. In 2016, Navas became the first Costa Rican player to win the UEFA Champions League after Real Madrid defeated neighbours Atlético in a penalty shoot-out in the final in Milan. A further world club title followed as well as a second successive Champions League triumph against Juventus in Cardiff last year.

FACTS AND FIGURES

Born: 15 December 1986
Position: Goalkeeper
Clubs: Deportivo Saprissa (CRC), Albacete (ESP), Levante (ESP), Real Madrid (ESP)
Caps (Goals): 74 (0)

"He was born on Mars or Venus or something. He's superhuman. He's given us so much. He's a leader on and off the pitch. We know that, with his saves, we will always get second chances."
Celso Borges, 2014 FIFA World Cup team-mate

STAR PLAYER

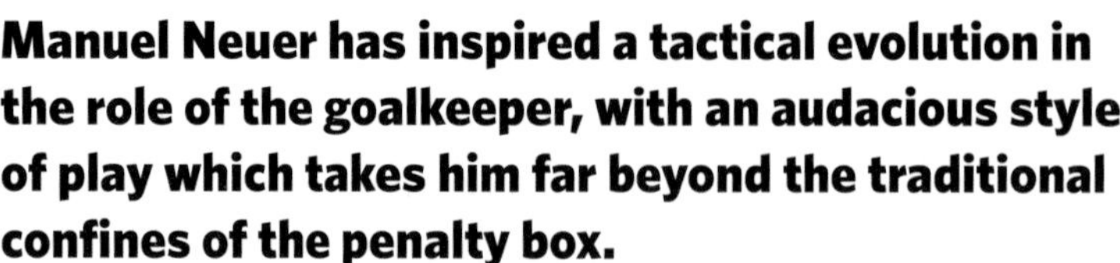

MANUEL NEUER

Manuel Neuer has inspired a tactical evolution in the role of the goalkeeper, with an audacious style of play which takes him far beyond the traditional confines of the penalty box.

Germany's 2014 FIFA World Cup winner has shown how goalkeepers - or "goalsweepers" - can add a valuable extra dimension to team play with their reading of the game and their confidence in using their feet in a positive style of attacking football.

Neuer, twice voted domestic Footballer of the Year, played for Germany's U-19s and then U-21s, with whom he won the UEFA European Championship in Sweden in 2009. Even before then, Neuer had been called into the senior national team by coach Joachim Löw, making his debut on an Asian tour against the United Arab Emirates.

A year later, Neuer was first choice when *Die Mannschaft* reached the semi-finals of 2010 FIFA World Cup in South Africa. He played all ten qualifying matches when Germany reached the finals of the 2012 UEFA European Championship and then all of their five ties up to the semi-finals in Poland and Ukraine.

After those two near-misses, Neuer tasted ultimate success at the 2014 FIFA World Cup in Brazil, where he played all seven of Germany's games up to, and including, the final victory over Argentina. An extra prize awaited Neuer at the Maracaña in Rio de Janeiro when he was handed the Golden Glove award as the finals' best goalkeeper.

Neuer enhanced his reputation at UEFA EURO 2016 in France when he saved two penalties in Germany's quarter-final victory over Italy in a penalty shoot-out. Subsequently, with the retirement of Bastian Schweinsteiger, he took over as his country's captain for the 2018 FIFA World Cup qualifying campaign.

Neuer made his name, and developed his modern playing style, with his local club FC Schalke 04 in Gelsenkirchen. With Schalke he won the German Cup once, and then enjoyed three more successive victories in the competition after transferring to Bayern Munich in 2011. By 2017, Neuer's safe hands had scooped up a further 11 titles at national and international level and earned him the status - among his many admirers - of the finest goalkeeper in the world.

"He is 'grandissimo'. He is physically strong and confident. He gives his team calmness with his aura, is great with the ball at his feet and makes impossible saves."
Gianluigi Buffon, former Italy goalkeeper and captain

FACTS AND FIGURES

Born: 27 March 1986
Position: Goalkeeper
Clubs: FC Schalke 04 (GER), Bayern Munich (GER)
Caps (Goals): 74 (0)

STAR PLAYER

NEYMAR

Neymar shoulders Brazil's dreams of seeing the *Selecão* triumph for a record-extending sixth time. It is a responsibility to which the world's most expensive player has grown accustomed.

Four years ago, Neymar da Silva Santos Júnior spearheaded Brazil's bid to make amends to their fans for their previous failure on home soil: the FIFA World Cup in 1950. Injury in the quarter-finals, however, meant Neymar missed the semi-final defeat by eventual champions Germany.

Two years later, the football dream was alive again. Neymar and his team-mates promised their fans that they would win a first Olympic title, in Rio de Janeiro. It all came down to the very last kick in the penalty shoot-out of the final game - and up stepped Neymar to fulfil his golden promise.

This was not Neymar's first national team success. He had shared in a South American Youth Championship victory in 2011, and then the FIFA Confederations Cup in 2013.

That was the year in which he transferred from Santos - Pelé's old club - to Barcelona. With Santos he had won five national and international titles; with Barcelona in Spain and Europe he won eight; and he has been maintaining the trophy hunt in France since his move to Paris Saint-Germain last year, for a world record €222m.

A shower of individual titles, including two awards as South American Footballer of the Year, and leading marksman awards have marked Neymar's explosive career since his Santos debut as a 17-year-old in early 2009. Neymar's skill, speed, poise and magic in front of goal soon had representatives of English and Spanish clubs brandishing big-money offers. In 2011 Neymar won the FIFA Puskás Award for the best goal of the year, in which he and Santos won the *Copa Libertadores* and reached the final of the FIFA Club World Cup.

Santos lost that final to Barcelona, who saw enough to prise Neymar away from Brazilian football in 2013. Until 2017, Barcelona's famed MSN attack - Messi, Suárez, Neymar - then wreaked havoc across the European club game before Neymar switched to PSG.

In the international game, he has maintained his transatlantic commute to lead Brazil's attack on the FIFA World Cup, the Summer Olympics and, now, the FIFA World Cup again.

FACTS AND FIGURES

Born: 5 February 1992
Position: Forward
Clubs: Santos (BRA), FC Barcelona (ESP), Paris Saint-Germain (FRA)
Caps (Goals): 83 (53)

"He's a complete player both for the team and because he scores the goals he does. He does it for Brazil and he does it for his clubs. Neymar is proof that the game is in good shape."
Pelé, Brazil's triple FIFA World Cup-winner

STAR PLAYER

PAUL POGBA

Paul Pogba will head into the FIFA World Cup™ finals with the status of the most expensive European footballer after his 2016 transfer from Juventus to Manchester United for £89m.

Pogba has been a permanent feature of French national teams all the way from his days as a highly promising youth player with the U-16s and subsequent promotion to captain of the U-19s, who reached the semi-finals of their European championship in 2012. Finally, in 2013, Pogba and his team-mates were on top of the world after winning the FIFA U-20 World Cup Leading by example, Pogba converted the first penalty in the 4-1 shoot-out victory over Uruguay after a 0-0 draw in the final.

Four months earlier, on 22 March 2013, Pogba had made his debut for the senior team, under coach Didier Deschamps, in a 3-1 victory against Georgia. His first goal for *Les Bleus* followed in a 4-2 win over Belarus. France defeated Ukraine in a play-off to bring Pogba, still only 21, onto the FIFA World Cup stage in 2014.

The Brazilian campaign saw Pogba voted man of the match after scoring the first goal in a victory over Nigeria in the round of 16. He was also voted the finals' best young player ahead of team-mate Raphaël Varane and Dutchman Memphis Depay.

On home soil, two years later, with France hosting, Pogba was a "leader" in the national team, who ended up as runners-up to Portugal in the UEFA European Championship.

This was Pogba's second finals setback in just over a year, he and Juventus having lost to Barcelona in the 2015 UEFA Champions League final. Pogba, who had originally made his name at Le Havre, joined Juventus in 2012 from Manchester United, having failed to make an early career breakthrough there. His transfer back to United in 2016, after the European Championship finals, was a form of homecoming.

Pogba won four Italian *Serie A* titles and the *Coppa Italia* twice with Juventus. Back at United, he further satisfied his trophy hunger last year by crowning his first season with success in both the UEFA Europa League and the EFL Cup.

FACTS AND FIGURES

Born: 15 March 1993
Position: Midfield
Clubs: Manchester United (ENG), Juventus (ITA), Manchester United (ENG)
Caps (Goals): 49 (8)

"Pogba is a special player, one of those who demand the ball all the time, whether the game is going well for his team or not. He never hides, he's just like Bobby Charlton that way."
Paddy Crerand, former Scotland midfielder

STAR PLAYER

CRISTIANO RONALDO

Cristiano Ronaldo dos Santos Aveiro ranks as one of the greatest players in football history thanks to his stand-alone achievements at all levels of the game: individual, club and national.

Portugal's captain has claimed five FIFA world player awards among a plethora of prizes. He has won the FIFA Club World Cup three times, the UEFA Champions League four times - with Manchester United and Real Madrid - and the UEFA European Championship in 2016.

The Madeira-born forward now has more than 600 goals in a lethal 16-year career that has taken him from Sporting Lisbon in Portugal to the pinnacle of the club game in England and Spain. He has set marksmanship records, including a stream of hat-tricks, in the UEFA Champions League and *La Liga*.

Portuguese fans have never seen a player like Ronaldo. Long ago he outstripped the goalscoring achievements of even Eusébio, the legend of the 1960s who inspired Portugal's finest FIFA World Cup finish of third place in 1966. His status was officially recognised in 2015 when he was named Portugal's best player of all time by the Portuguese FA.

Ronaldo was 18 when he made his debut against Kazakhstan in August 2003. He is now the record-holder in terms of both international appearances and goals. Ronaldo has also led Portugal into the finals of seven major tournaments, starting with UEFA EURO 2004, when the hosts finished as runners-up.

Two years later, Ronaldo's first FIFA World Cup foray saw his team finish fourth in Germany. In 2010, Portugal lost in the round of 16 to a Spanish team whose stars Ronaldo knew only too well. Brazil 2014 was a further disappointment: Ronaldo was hampered by injury, and Portugal fell in the first round.

His personal qualities and those of his team-mates were underlined, however, in 2016 when Portugal won the UEFA European Championship. Ronaldo, having scored three goals, was injured early in the final but remained a force in the match with his touchline encouragement. His reward, as captain, was then to hoist aloft Portugal's first senior trophy.

Now to maybe crown his career at the FIFA World Cup ...

FACTS AND FIGURES

Born: 5 February 1985
Position: Forward
Clubs: Sporting Lisbon (POR), Manchester United (ENG), Real Madrid (ESP)
Caps (Goals): 147 (79)

"He is the best and he's amazing at what he does. He is always looking to win titles. Even in a training session he wants to win. He has something inside. He is a born leader."
Zinédine Zidane, Real Madrid coach

STAR PLAYER

MOHAMED SALAH

Mohamed Salah has proved himself one of Egypt's most outstanding exports, and the *Pharaohs* are now relying on him to light up their long-awaited return to the FIFA World Cup™ finals.

The high-speed winger launched his career as a teenager with El Mokawloon and moved to Europe to join Swiss club Basel in 2012.

The Port Said Stadium riot, which led to the tragic deaths of 74 people, had prompted the suspension of the domestic league, so the Egyptian U-23 team undertook a foreign tour. Salah impressed Basel after starring there in a friendly match.

He made his competitive debut in the UEFA Champions League preliminary stages, and his goals helped Basel to league championship success. In January 2014, Salah was sold to Chelsea for £11m, but his stay in London lasted for only 12 months. In the middle of an English Premier League title-winning run, he was loaned to Italy's Serie A, first to Fiorentina and then Roma.

A permanent transfer to Roma followed and then more goals and individual awards, which persuaded Liverpool to buy Salah last year for a near club record £34m and to bring even more firepower to an exciting Anfield attack. At the same time, Salah had been proving himself an increasingly important member of the Egyptian national team in both the FIFA World Cup and the CAF Africa Cup of Nations.

Salah played for the Egyptian U-20s and U-23s, which included appearances at the FIFA U-20 World Cup in 2011 and the football tournament at the Summer Olympics in London the following year. In between, Salah made his senior national team debut against Sierra Leone. He scored a hat-trick against Zimbabwe in the 2014 FIFA World Cup qualifiers, but his six goals overall were not enough to take the *Pharaohs* to Brazil for the finals.

Last year, Salah was voted into the official team of the tournament as Egypt finished runners-up in the Cup of Nations in Gabon. He was then Egypt's leading marksman, with five goals, in the campaign that returned them to the FIFA World Cup finals for the first time in 28 years.

FACTS AND FIGURES

Born: 15 June 1992
Position: Winger
Clubs: El Mokawloon (EGY), Basel (SUI), Chelsea (ENG), Fiorentina (ITA), Roma (ITA), Liverpool (ENG)
Caps (Goals): 56 (32)

"When Salah plays well, then his teams play well. He has developed physically and in game intelligence and makes all his opponents worry about how to try to stop him."
Mohamed Aboutrika, former Egypt playmaker

STAR PLAYER

LUIS SUÁREZ

Luis Suárez is one of the world's finest centre-forwards and has proved the point time and again, not only with Uruguay but with major clubs such as Ajax, Liverpool and Barcelona.

FACTS AND FIGURES

Born: 24 January 1987
Position: Centre-forward
Clubs: Nacional (URU), Groningen (NED), Ajax (NED), Liverpool (ENG), FC Barcelona (ESP)
Caps (Goals): 95 (49)

The 31-year-old from Salto in the double FIFA World Cup-winning South American nation started his honours pursuit early. He was a Uruguayan league champion with Nacional of Montevideo before making a courageous and ambitious transfer, aged 19, to Dutch club Groningen.

A year later he joined former world and European champions Ajax. His leadership qualities and natural goalscoring ability quickly saw him become captain and league top scorer. He also shot his way to more than 100 club goals to rank alongside Ajax legends such as Johan Cruyff, Marco van Basten and Dennis Bergkamp. His cascade of goals over four seasons secured a transfer to Liverpool and a further 82 goals in all competitions before his move to Barcelona in 2014 after the FIFA World Cup in Brazil.

Suárez has won more than a dozen national and international titles at club level, but his fierce will to win has brought him controversy. He has been suspended three times for biting opponents, including at the 2014 FIFA World Cup when Uruguay reached the round of 16.

Suárez made his debut in the light blue of *La Celeste* at the FIFA U-20 World Cup in 2007 and was promoted to join the senior national squad that same year for a friendly against Colombia. He was a stalwart of the team who finished fourth at the 2010 FIFA World Cup, though he missed the semi-final defeat by the Netherlands, after a red card for conceding a penalty in the quarter-final victory over Ghana.

Suárez bounced back a year later when he was voted player of the tournament after leading Uruguay to victory in the 2011 *Copa América*. At the FIFA World Cup in Brazil, Suárez claimed his 40th goal for the national team but missed their round-of-16 defeat to Colombia due to a further suspension. Only team-mate Edinson Cavani, with 40 goals by the end of the qualifying campaign, comes anywhere near Suárez in terms of attacking danger as Uruguay head for Russia.

"He has been getting better with every successive transfer to a new club. His value is not only in the goals he scores but his ability to unbalance any defence. He is the complete player."
Enzo Francescoli, former Uruguayan FIFA World Cup star

FIFA World Cup™ Records

The FIFA World Cup™ offers an enduring attraction for fans: since the inaugural event in Uruguay in 1930, the matches played while qualifying and competing have thrown up a multiplicity of facts, figures and statistics through the years. Some records last longer than others – notably Frenchman Just Fontaine's feat in scoring 13 goals in the 1958 tournament in Sweden.

LEFT: (left to right) Brazil's Rivaldo, Ronaldo and Cafu celebrate FIFA World Cup success in Yokohama in 2002.

TEAM RECORDS

Some countries are regulars on the biggest footballing stage of all and eight have experienced the thrill of being crowned the best team in the world, while others have seized the chance to secure a place in the history books with special achievements.

FIFA WORLD CUP™ FINALS

Year	Hosts	Winners	Runners-up	Score
1930	Uruguay	Uruguay	Argentina	4-2
1934	Italy	Italy	Czechoslovakia	2-1 (a.e.t.)
1938	France	Italy	Hungary	4-2
1950	Brazil	Uruguay	Brazil	2-1
1954	Switzerland	West Germany	Hungary	3-2
1958	Sweden	Brazil	Sweden	5-2
1962	Chile	Brazil	Czechoslovakia	3-1
1966	England	England	West Germany	4-2 (a.e.t.)
1970	Mexico	Brazil	Italy	4-1
1974	West Germany	West Germany	Netherlands	2-1
1978	Argentina	Argentina	Netherlands	3-1 (a.e.t.)
1982	Spain	Italy	West Germany	3-1
1986	Mexico	Argentina	West Germany	3-2
1990	Italy	West Germany	Argentina	1-0
1994	USA	Brazil	Italy	0-0 (a.e.t.; 3-2 on pens)
1998	France	France	Brazil	3-0
2002	Japan/Korea Republic	Brazil	Germany	2-0
2006	Germany	Italy	France	1-1 (a.e.t.; 5-3 on pens)
2010	South Africa	Spain	Netherlands	1-0 (a.e.t.)
2014	Brazil	Germany	Argentina	1-0 (a.e.t.)

LEFT: History being made at the inaugural FIFA World Cup in the Estadio Centenario in Montevideo in 1930.

OPPOSITE TOP: Germany celebrate their fourth FIFA World Cup triumph (the first three had been as West Germany), in Rio de Janeiro's Estádio do Maracaña in 2014.

MOST FIFA WORLD CUP™ FINAL VICTORIES

5	Brazil
4	Italy
=	Germany
2	Argentina
=	Uruguay
1	England
=	France
=	Spain

MOST FIFA WORLD CUP™ FINAL APPEARANCES

8	Germany
7	Brazil
6	Italy
5	Argentina
3	Netherlands
2	Czechoslovakia
=	France
=	Hungary
=	Uruguay
1	England
=	Sweden

FIFA WORLD CUP™ ALL-TIME RANKING

		Finals	P	W	D	L	Gls For	Gls Agst	Gls Ave	Points
1	Brazil	20	104	70	17	17	221	102	2.2	227
2	Germany	18	106	66	20	20	224	121	2.1	218
3	Italy	18	83	45	21	17	128	77	1.9	156
4	Argentina	16	77	42	14	21	131	84	1.8	140
5	Spain	14	59	29	12	18	92	66	1.7	99

MOST FIFA WORLD CUP™ FINALS TOURNAMENT APPEARANCES

20	Brazil
18	Germany
=	Italy
16	Argentina
15	Mexico

FIFA WORLD CUP™ FINAL ATTENDANCES

1930:	93,000	(Estadio Centenario, Montevideo)
1934:	45,000	(Stadio Nazionale del PNF, Rome)
1938:	60,000	(Stade Olympique de Colombes, Paris)
1950:	173,830-210,000	(Estádio do Maracaña, Rio de Janeiro)
1954:	64,000	(Wankdorfstadion, Berne)
1958:	51,800	(Rasunda Fotbollstadion, Solna)
1962:	68,679	(Estadio Nacional, Santiago)
1966:	98,000	(Wembley Stadium, London)
1970:	107,412	(Estadio Azteca, Mexico City)
1974:	75,200	(Olympiastadion, Munich)
1978:	71,483	(Estadio Monumental, Buenos Aires)
1982:	90,000	(Estadio Santiago Bernabéu, Madrid)
1986:	114,600	(Estadio Azteca, Mexico City)
1990:	73,603	(Stadio Olimpico, Rome)
1994:	94,194	(Rose Bowl, Pasadena)
1998:	75,000	(Stade de France, Paris)
2002:	69,029	(International Stadium, Yokohama)
2006:	69,000	(Olympiastadion, Berlin)
2010:	84,490	(Soccer City, Johannesburg)
2014:	74,738	(Estádio do Maracaña, Rio de Janeiro)

OVERALL TOURNAMENT ATTENDANCES

1930:	434,500	(24,139 average)
1934:	395,000	(21,059)
1938:	483,000	(26,833)
1950:	1,337,000	(47,091)
1954:	943,000	(34,212)
1958:	868,000	(26,274)
1962:	776,000	(28,096)
1966:	1,614,677	(51,094)
1970:	1,673,975	(50,124)
1974:	1,774,022	(46,685)
1978:	1,610,215	(40,688)
1982:	1,856,277	(40,572)
1986:	2,407,431	(46,026)
1990:	2,517,348	(48,391)
1994:	3,587,538	(68,991)
1998:	2,785,100	(43,517)
2002:	2,705,197	(42,269)
2006:	3,352,605	(52,401)
2010:	3,178,856	(49,670)
2014:	3,386,810	(52,919)
Total:	37,686,551	(45,079)

LEFT: A crowd of 94,194 was in the Rose Bowl at Pasadena, California, to watch Brazil and Italy play in the 1994 FIFA World Cup USA Final.

PLAYER RECORDS

Appearing at the FIFA World Cup™ finals is the pinnacle of a footballing career for most players and some have been fortunate enough to savour the experience on several occasions, while others have made an appearance very early or towards the end of their career.

MOST FIFA WORLD CUP™ FINALS TOURNAMENTS

These players attended five World Cup finals tournaments

5	Gianluigi Buffon	(Italy) 1998, 2002, 2006, 2010, 2014
=	Antonio Carbajal	(Mexico) 1950, 1954, 1958, 1962, 1966
=	Lothar Matthäus	(West Germany/Germany) 1982, 1986, 1990, 1994, 1998

BELOW LEFT: Italy's Gianluigi Buffon was first included in Italy's squad for the 1998 finals, but did not play.

BELOW: Lothar Matthäus captained West Germany to victory in 1990.

MOST APPEARANCES IN WORLD CUP FINALS MATCHES

25	Lothar Matthäus (West Germany/Germany)
24	Miroslav Klose (Germany)
23	Paolo Maldini (Italy)
21	Diego Maradona (Argentina)
=	Uwe Seeler (West Germany)
=	Wladyslaw Zmuda (Poland)

ABOVE: Northern Ireland's Norman Whiteside is the youngest player to appear in the finals.

YOUNGEST PLAYERS TO PLAY IN THE WORLD CUP FINAL

Pelé	(Brazil)	17 years, 249 days in 1958
Giuseppe Bergomi	(Italy)	18 years, 201 days in 1982
Ruben Moran	(Uruguay)	19 years, 344 days in 1950

YOUNGEST PLAYERS AT THE WORLD CUP FINALS

Norman Whiteside	(N Ireland)	17 years, 41 days in 1982
Samuel Eto'o	(Cameroon)	17 years, 99 days in 1998
Femi Opabunmi	(Nigeria)	17 years, 101 days in 2002

OLDEST PLAYERS IN THE WORLD CUP FINAL

Dino Zoff	(Italy)	40 years, 133 days in 1982
Gunnar Gren	(Sweden)	37 years, 241 days in 1958
Jan Jongbloed	(Netherlands)	37 years, 212 days in 1974

OLDEST PLAYERS AT THE WORLD CUP FINALS

Faryd Mondragón	(Colombia)	43 years, 3 days in 2014
Roger Milla	(Cameroon)	42 years, 39 days in 1994
Pat Jennings	(N Ireland)	41 years in 1986

UNBEATEN GOALKEEPERS IN THE FIFA WORLD CUP™ FINALS

Walter Zenga	(Italy)	517 minutes without conceding a goal, 1990
Peter Shilton	(England)	502 minutes, 1986-1990
Sepp Maier	(West Germany)	475 minutes, 1974-78

OFFICIAL BEST GOALKEEPER OF THE TOURNAMENT

1930	Enrique Ballestreros	(Uruguay)
1934	Ricardo Zamora	(Spain)
1938	František Plánícka	(Czechoslovakia)
1950	Roque Máspoli	(Uruguay)
1954	Gyula Grosics	(Hungary)
1958	Harry Gregg	(Northern Ireland)
1962	Viliam Schrojf	(Czechoslovakia)
1966	Gordon Banks	(England)
1970	Ladislao Mazurkiewicz	(Uruguay)
1974	Jan Tomaszewski	(Poland)
1978	Ubaldo Fillol	(Argentina)
1982	Dino Zoff	(Italy)
1986	Harald Schumacher	(West Germany)
1990	Sergio Goycoechea	(Argentina)
1994	Michel Preud'homme	(Belgium)
1998	Fabien Barthez	(France)
2002	Oliver Kahn	(Germany)
2006	Gianluigi Buffon	(Italy)
2010	Iker Casillas	(Spain)
2014	Manuel Neuer	(Germany)

DOUBLE WINNERS

Players to appear on the winning side in two World Cup finals

Cafu	(Brazil)	1994, 2002
Didi	(Brazil)	1958, 1962
Giovanni Ferrari	(Italy)	1934, 1938
Garrincha	(Brazil)	1958, 1962
Gilmar	(Brazil)	1958, 1962
Giuseppe Meazza	(Italy)	1934, 1938
Pelé	(Brazil)	1958, 1970
Djalma Santos	(Brazil)	1958, 1962
Nílton Santos	(Brazil)	1958, 1962
Vavá	(Brazil)	1958, 1962
Zagallo	(Brazil)	1958, 1962
Zito	(Brazil)	1958, 1962

GOALSCORING RECORDS

The old adage is that "goals win matches" and most fans come to watch goals being scored. Most FIFA World Cup™ record-breaking goalscorers become legends overnight but others just enjoy one day in the sun.

TOP-SCORING TEAMS IN EACH FIFA WORLD CUP™ FINALS

Year	Team	Goals
1930	Argentina	18 (5 matches)
1934	Italy	12 (5 matches)
1938	Hungary	15 (4 matches)
1950	Brazil	22 (6 matches)
1954	Hungary	27 (5 matches)
1958	France	23 (6 matches)
1962	Brazil	14 (6 matches)
1966	Portugal	17 (6 matches)
1970	Brazil	19 (6 matches)
1974	Poland	16 (7 matches)
1978	Argentina/Netherlands	15 (7 matches)
1982	Brazil	15 (5 matches)
1986	Argentina	14 (7 matches)
1990	West Germany	15 (7 matches)
1994	Sweden	15 (7 matches)
1998	France	15 (7 matches)
2002	Brazil	18 (7 matches)
2006	Germany	14 (7 matches)
2010	Germany	16 (7 matches)
2014	Germany	18 (7 matches)

TOTAL GOALS IN EACH FIFA WORLD CUP™ FINALS

Year	Total Goals	Goals per Match
1930	70	(3.89 per match)
1934	70	(4.12 per match)
1938	84	(4.67 per match)
1950	88	(4.00 per match)
1954	140	(5.38 per match)
1958	126	(3.60 per match)
1962	89	(2.78 per match)
1966	89	(2.78 per match)
1970	95	(2.97 per match)
1974	97	(2.55 per match)
1978	102	(2.68 per match)
1982	146	(2.81 per match)
1986	132	(2.54 per match)
1990	115	(2.21 per match)
1994	141	(2.71 per match)
1998	171	(2.67 per match)
2002	161	(2.52 per match)
2006	147	(2.30 per match)
2010	145	(2.26 per match)
2014	171	(2.67 per match)

MOST GOALS BY TEAM IN A SINGLE FIFA WORLD CUP™ FINALS

Goals	Team	Year
27	Hungary	(1954)
25	West Germany	(1954)
23	France	(1958)
22	Brazil	(1950)
19	Brazil	(1970)

MOST GOALS BY TEAMS IN FIFA WORLD CUP™ FINALS (100 PLUS)

224	West Germany/Germany
221	Brazil
131	Argentina
128	Italy

RIGHT: Nandor Hidegkuti (third right) scored two goals in Hungary's 8-3 defeat of West Germany in a 1954 FIFA World Cup Group B match in Basel.

BIGGEST FIFA WORLD CUP™ FINALS WINS

Hungary	10-1	El Salvador	(1982)
Hungary	9-0	South Korea	(1954)
Yugoslavia	9-0	Zaire	(1974)
Sweden	8-0	Cuba	(1938)
Uruguay	8-0	Bolivia	(1950)
Germany	8-0	Saudi Arabia	(2002)
Turkey	7-0	Korea Republic	(1954)
Uruguay	7-0	Scotland	(1954)
Poland	7-0	Haiti	(1974)
Portugal	7-0	Korea DPR	(2010)

SINGLE-TOURNAMENT TOP SCORERS

13	Just Fontaine	(France)	1958
11	Sándor Kocsis	(Hungary)	1954
10	Gerd Müller	(West Germany)	1970

FIFA WORLD CUP™ FINALS ALL-TIME LEADING GOALSCORERS

Goals	Name	(Country)	Tournaments	Matches
16	Miroslav Klose	(Germany)	2002, 2006, 2010, 2014	(24)
15	Ronaldo	(Brazil)	1998, 2002, 2006	(19)
14	Gerd Müller	(West Germany)	1970, 1974	(13)
13	Just Fontaine	(France)	1958	(6)
12	Pelé	(Brazil)	1958, 1962, 1966, 1970	(14)
11	Sándor Kocsis	(Hungary)	1954	(5)
11	Jürgen Klinsmann	(West Germany/ Germany)	1990, 1994, 1998	(17)
10	Helmut Rahn	(West Germany)	1954, 1958	(10)
10	Teófilo Cubillas	(Peru)	1970, 1978, 1982	(13)
10	Grzegorz Lato	(Poland)	1974, 1978, 1982	(20)
10	Gary Lineker	(England)	1986, 1990	(12)
10	Gabriel Batistuta	(Argentina)	1994, 1998, 2002	(12)
10	Thomas Müller	(Germany)	2010, 2014	(13)

ALL FIFA WORLD CUP™ FINALS TOURNAMENT TOP SCORERS

1930 (Uruguay)	Guillermo Stábile	Argentina	8
1934 (Italy)	Oldřich Nejedlý	Czechoslovakia	5
1938 (France)	Leônidas	Brazil	7
1950 (Brazil)	Ademir	Brazil	8
1954 (Switzerland)	Sándor Kocsis	Hungary	11
1958 (Sweden)	Just Fontaine	France	13
1962 (Chile)	Garrincha	Brazil	4
=	Vavá	Brazil	4
=	Leonel Sánchez	Chile	4
=	Flórián Albert	Hungary	4
=	Valentin Ivanov	Soviet Union	4
=	Dražan Jerković	Yugoslavia	4
1966 (England)	Eusébio	Portugal	9
1970 (Mexico)	Gerd Müller	Germany	10
1974 (West Germany)	Grzegorz Lato	Poland	7
1978 (Argentina)	Mario Kempes	Argentina	6
1982 (Spain)	Paolo Rossi	Italy	6
1986 (Mexico)	Gary Lineker	England	6
1990 (Italy)	Salvatore Schillaci	Italy	6
1994 (United States)	Hristo Stoichkov	Bulgaria	6
=	Oleg Salenko	Russia	6
1998 (France)	Davor Šuker	Croatia	6
2002 (Japan/Korea Republic)	Ronaldo	Brazil	8
2006 (Germany)	Miroslav Klose	Germany	5
2010 (South Africa)	Thomas Müller	Germany	5
=	David Villa	Spain	5
=	Wesley Sneijder	Netherlands	5
=	Diego Forlán	Uruguay	5
2014 (Brazil)	James Rodríguez	Colombia	6

BELOW: Brazil's Ronaldo was eight-goal top scorer in 2002.

PENALTY SHOOT-OUTS BY COUNTRY

5	Argentina	(4 wins, 1 defeat)
4	Germany	(4 wins)
4	Brazil	(3 wins, 1 defeat)
4	France	(2 wins, 2 defeats)
4	Italy	(1 win, 3 defeats)
3	Netherlands	(1 win, 2 defeats)
3	Spain	(1 win, 2 defeats)
3	England	(3 defeats)
2	Rep. of Ireland	(1 win, 1 defeat)
2	Costa Rica	(1 win, 1 defeat)
2	Mexico	(2 defeats)
2	Romania	(2 defeats)
1	14 other nations	

OTHER RECORDS

Managing the winning nation at the FIFA World Cup™ is the greatest possible career achievement for any coach. It is also such a challenge that only one man, Italy's Vittorio Pozzo, has managed it twice.

FIFA WORLD CUP™ WINNING COACHES

1930	Alberto Suppici	(Uruguay)
1934	Vittorio Pozzo	(Italy)
1938	Vittorio Pozzo	(Italy)
1950	Juan López	(Uruguay)
1954	Sepp Herberger	(West Germany)
1958	Vicente Feola	(Brazil)
1962	Aymoré Moreira	(Brazil)
1966	Alf Ramsey	(England)
1970	Mário Zagallo	(Brazil)
1974	Helmut Schön	(West Germamy)
1978	César Luis Menotti	(Argentina)
1982	Enzo Bearzot	(Italy)
1986	Carlos Bilardo	(Argentina)
1990	Franz Beckenbauer	(West Germany)
1994	Carlos Alberto Parreira	(Brazil)
1998	Aimé Jacquet	(France)
2002	Luiz Felipe Scolari	(Brazil)
2006	Marcello Lippi	(Italy)
2010	Vicente del Bosque	(Spain)
2014	Joachim Löw	(Germany)

FIFA WORLD CUP™ FINAL REFEREES

1930	Jean Langenus	(Belgium)
1934	Ivan Eklind	(Sweden)
1938	Georges Capdeville	(France)
1950	George Reader	(England)
1954	William Ling	(England)
1958	Maurice Guigue	(France)
1962	Nikolay Latyshev	(USSR)
1966	Gottfried Dienst	(Switzerland)
1970	Rudi Glöckner	(West Germany)
1974	Jack Taylor	(England)
1978	Sergio Gonella	(Italy)
1982	Arnaldo Cézar Coelho	(Brazil)
1986	Romualdo Arppi Filho	(Brazil)
1990	Edgardo Codesal	(Mexico)
1994	Sándor Puhl	(Hungary)
1998	Said Belqola	(Morocco)
2002	Pierluigi Collina	(Italy)
2006	Horacio Elizondo	(Argentina)
2010	Howard Webb	(England)
2014	Nicola Rizzoli	(Italy)

MOST MATCHES OFFICIATED BY FIFA WORLD CUP™ REFEREES

Ravshan Irmatov	(Uzbekistan)	nine games	(2010, 2014)
Benito Archundia	(Mexico)	eight games	(2006, 2010)
Jorge Larrionda	(Uruguay)	eight games	(2006, 2010)
Joël Quiniou	(France)	eight games	(1986, 1990, 1994)
Ali Mohamed Bujsaim	(UAE)	seven games	(1994, 1998, 2002)
Frank de Bleeckere	(Belgium)	seven games	(2006, 2010)
Juan Gardezábal	(Spain)	seven games	(1958, 1962, 1966)
Mervyn Griffiths	(Wales)	seven games	(1950, 1954, 1958)
Jean Langenus	(Belgium)	seven games	(1930, 1934, 1938)
Marco Antonio Rodríguez	(Mexico)	seven games	(2006, 2010, 2014)
Carlos Eugênio Simon	(Brazil)	seven games	(2002, 2006, 2010)
Gamal Al-Ghandour	(Egypt)	six games	(1998, 2002)
Jamal Al Sharif	(Syria)	six games	(1986, 1990, 1994)
Arturo Brizio Carter	(Mexico)	six games	(1994, 1998)
Ivan Eklind	(Sweden)	six games	(1934, 1950)
Arthur Ellis	(England)	six games	(1950, 1954, 1958)
Nikolay Latyshev	(Soviet Union)	six games	(1958, 1962)
Roberto Roselli	(Italy)	six games	(2006, 2010)
Oscar Ruiz	(Colombia)	six games	(2002, 2006, 2010)

FIFA WORLD CUP™ RED CARDS, BY COUNTRY

10	Argentina
9	Brazil
7	Cameroon, Italy
6	Czechoslovakia/Czech Republic, Germany/West Germany, Mexico, Netherlands, Uruguay
5	France, Hungary
4	Portugal, Yugoslavia/Serbia, USA
3	Bulgaria, Croatia, Denmark, England, Soviet Union/Russia, Sweden
2	Australia, Belgium, Bolivia, Chile, Paraguay, Korea Republic, Turkey
1	Angola, Austria, Canada, China PR, Côte d'Ivoire, Ghana, Honduras, Iraq, Jamaica, Northern Ireland, Peru, Poland, Romania, Saudi Arabia, Scotland, Senegal, Slovenia, South Africa, Spain, Togo, Trinidad & Tobago, Tunisia, Ukraine, United Arab Emirates, Zaire

FIFA WORLD CUP™ FINALS RED CARDS

1930	1
1934	1
1938	4
1950	0
1954	3
1958	3
1962	6
1966	5
1970	0
1974	5
1978	3
1982	5
1986	8
1990	16
1994	15
1998	22
2002	17
2006	28
2010	17
2014	10

FASTEST RED CARDS IN FIFA WORLD CUP™ FINALS TOURNAMENTS

1 min:	José Batista	(Uruguay)	v	Scotland	1986
3 min:	Marco Etcheverry*	(Bolivia)	v	Germany	1994
=	Ion Vladoiu*	(Romania)	v	Switzerland	1994
=	Morten Wieghorst*	(Denmark)	v	South Africa	1998
6 min:	Lauren*	(Cameroon)	v	Chile	1998
8 min:	Giorgio Ferrini	(Italy)	v	Chile	1962
=	Miklos Molnar*	(Denmark)	v	South Africa	1998

These are the number of minutes the players were on the pitch. * = Substitutes' time after coming on.

MOST CARDS IN ONE MATCH

20 (four red and 16 yellow):	Portugal	v	Netherlands	(2006)

QUALIFYING COMPETITION

The number of countries entering each qualifying competition

World Cup	Teams entering qualifiers
Uruguay 1930	-
Italy 1934	32
France 1938	37
Brazil 1950	34
Switzerland 1954	45
Sweden 1958	55
Chile 1962	56
England 1966	74
Mexico 1970	75
West Germany 1974	99
Argentina 1978	107
Spain 1982	109
Mexico 1986	121
Italy 1990	116
USA 1994	147
France 1998	174
Japan/Korea Republic 2002	199
Germany 2006	198
South Africa 2010	204
Brazil 2014	207

BEST PLAYERS OF THE TOURNAMENT (Golden Ball)

1930	José Nasazzi	Uruguay
1934	Giuseppe Meazza	Italy
1938	Leônidas	Brazil
1950	Zizinho	Brazil
1954	Ferenc Puskás	Hungary
1958	Didi	Brazil
1962	Garrincha	Brazil
1966	Bobby Charlton	England
1970	Pelé	Brazil
1974	Johan Cruyff	Netherlands
1978	Mario Kempes	Argentina
1982	Paolo Rossi	Italy
1986	Diego Maradona	Argentina
1990	Salvatore Schillaci	Italy
1994	Romário	Brazil
1998	Ronaldo	Brazil
2002	Oliver Kahn	Germany
2006	Zinédine Zidane	France
2010	Diego Forlán	Uruguay
2014	Lionel Messi	Argentina

FIFA WORLD CUP™ QUALIFICATION COMPETITION RECORD

Team	Tnts	P	W	D	L	GF	GA
Portugal	20	139	76	33	30	262	139
United States	18	154	77	36	41	266	181
Netherlands	18	125	82	24	19	296	93
Spain	18	117	81	25	11	276	76
Mexico	16	175	113	37	25	436	126
Costa Rica	16	172	85	43	44	295	176
Australia	14	139	81	35	23	359	112
Korea Republic	14	135	82	36	17	264	86
Argentina	13	136	75	36	25	235	127
Brazil	12	110	68	30	12	240	70

TOP WINS IN FIFA WORLD CUP™ QUALIFIERS

1	Australia	31-0	American Samoa	11 April 2001
2	Australia	22-0	Tonga	9 April 2001
3	Maldives	0-17	Iran	2 June 1997
4	Australia	13-0	Solomon Islands	11 June 1997
	New Zealand	13-0	Fiji	16 August 1981
	Fiji	13-0	American Samoa	7 April 2001
7	Syria	12-0	Maldives	4 June 1997
	Maldives	0-12	Syria	9 June 1997
9	West Germany	12-0	Cyprus	21 May 1969
10	Australia	11-0	Samoa	16 April 2001
	Mexico	11-0	St Vincent	6 December 1992

UNSUCCESSFUL HOSTING BIDS

1930:	Hungary, Italy, Netherlands, Spain, Sweden
1934:	Sweden
1938:	Argentina, Germany
1950:	None
1954:	None
1958:	None
1962:	Argentina, West Germany
1966:	Spain, West Germany
1970:	Argentina
1974:	Spain
1978:	Mexico
1982:	West Germany
1986:	Colombia (won rights, but later withdrew), Canada, USA
1990:	England, Greece, USSR
1994:	Brazil, Morocco
1998:	Morocco, Switzerland
2002:	Mexico
2006:	Brazil, England, Morocco, South Africa
2010:	Egypt, Libya, Morocco, Tunisia
2014:	None
2018:	England, Netherlands/Belgium, Spain/Portugal

TEAMS WITH MOST CARDS IN FINALS

120	Argentina
117	Germany
108	Brazil
98	Italy
97	Netherlands

2018 FIFA WORLD CUP RUSSIA™ MATCH GUIDE

GROUP A

14 June, 18:00	Russia	5	0	Saudi Arabia	Moscow (Luzhniki)
15 June, 17:00	Egypt	0	1	Uruguay	Ekaterinburg
19 June, 21:00	Russia	3	1	Egypt	Saint Petersburg
20 June, 18:00	Uruguay	1	0	Saudi Arabia	Rostov-on-Don
25 June, 18:00	Uruguay			Russia	Samara
25 June, 17:00	Saudi Arabia			Egypt	Volgograd

Team	P	W	D	L	GD	Pts
Russia						
Uruguay						
Egypt						
Saudi Arabia						

GROUP B

15 June, 21:00	Portugal	3	3	Spain	Sochi
15 June, 18:00	Morocco	0	1	IR Iran	Saint Petersburg
20 June, 15:00	Portugal	1	0	Morocco	Moscow (Luzhniki)
20 June, 21:00	IR Iran	0	1	Spain	Kazan
25 June, 21:00	IR Iran			Portugal	Saransk
25 June, 20:00	Spain			Morocco	Kaliningrad

Team	P	W	D	L	GD	Pts
Portugal						
Spain						
Morocco						
Iran						

GROUP C

16 June, 13:00	France	2	1	Australia	Kazan
16 June, 19:00	Peru	0	1	Denmark	Saransk
21 June,20:00	France			Peru	Ekaterinburg
21 June, 16:00	Denmark			Australia	Samara
26 June, 17:00	Denmark			France	Moscow (Luzhniki)
26 June, 17:00	Australia			Peru	Sochi

Team	P	W	D	L	GD	Pts

GROUP D

16 June, 16:00	Argentina	1	1	Iceland	Moscow (Spartak)
16 June, 21:00	Croatia	2	0	Nigeria	Kaliningrad
21 June, 21:00	Argentina			Croatia	Nizhny Novgorod
22 June, 18:00	Nigeria			Iceland	Volgograd
26 June, 21:00	Nigeria			Argentina	Saint Petersburg
26 June, 21:00	Iceland			Croatia	Rostov-on-Don

Team	P	W	D	L	GD	Pts

GROUP E

17 June, 21:00	Brazil	1	1	Switzerland	Rostov-on-Don
17 June, 16:00	Costa Rica	0	1	Serbia	Samara
22 June, 15:00	Brazil			Costa Rica	Saint Petersburg
22 June, 20:00	Serbia			Switzerland	Kaliningrad
27 June, 21:00	Serbia			Brazil	Moscow (Spartak)
27 June, 21:00	Switzerland			Costa Rica	Nizhny Novgorod

Team	P	W	D	L	GD	Pts

GROUP F

17 June, 18:00	Germany	0	1	Mexico	Moscow (Luzhniki)
18 June, 15:00	Sweden	1	0	Korea Republic	Nizhny Novgorod
23 June, 21:00	Germany			Sweden	Sochi
23 June, 18:00	Korea Republic			Mexico	Rostov-on-Don
27 June, 17:00	Korea Republic			Germany	Kazan
27 June, 19:00	Mexico			Sweden	Ekaterinburg

Team	P	W	D	L	GD	Pts

GROUP G

18 June, 18:00	Belgium			Panama	Sochi
18 June, 21:00	Tunisia			England	Volgograd
23 June, 15:00	Belgium			Tunisia	Moscow (Spartak)
24 June, 15:00	England			Panama	Nizhny Novgorod
28 June, 20:00	England			Belgium	Kaliningrad
28 June, 21:00	Panama			Tunisia	Saransk

Team	P	W	D	L	GD	Pts

GROUP H

19 June, 18:00	Poland			Senegal	Moscow (Spartak)
19 June, 15:00	Colombia			Japan	Saransk
24 June, 21:00	Poland			Colombia	Kazan
24 June, 20:00	Japan			Senegal	Ekaterinburg
28 June, 17:00	Japan			Poland	Volgograd
28 June, 18:00	Senegal			Colombia	Samara

Team	P	W	D	L	GD	Pts

ROUND OF 16

30 June, 21:00	WINNER A			RUNNER-UP B	Sochi
30 June, 17:00	WINNER C			RUNNER-UP D	Kazan
1 July, 17:00	WINNER B			RUNNER-UP A	Moscow (Luzhniki)
1 July, 21:00	WINNER D			RUNNER-UP C	Nizhny Novgorod
2 July, 18:00	WINNER E			RUNNER-UP F	Samara
2 July, 21:00	WINNER G			RUNNER-UP H	Rostov-on-Don
3 July, 17:00	WINNER F			RUNNER-UP E	Saint Petersburg
3 July, 21:00	WINNER H			RUNNER-UP G	Moscow (Spartak)

QUARTER-FINALS

6 July, 17:00	WINNER 1			WINNER 2	Nizhny Novgorod
6 July, 21:00	WINNER 5			WINNER 6	Kazan
7 July, 21:00	WINNER 3			WINNER 4	Sochi
7 July, 18:00	WINNER 7			WINNER 8	Samara

SEMI-FINALS

10 July, 21:00	WINNER A			WINNER B	Saint Petersburg
11 July, 21:00	WINNER C			WINNER D	Moscow (Luzhniki)

THIRD-PLACE PLAY-OFF

14 July, 17:00					Saint Petersburg

2018 FIFA WORLD CUP™ FINAL

15 July, 18:00					Moscow (Luzhniki)

Note: Local kick-off times for Kaliningrad UTC +2; Samara UTC +4; Ekaterinburg UTC +5; Moscow and all other venues UTC +3.

PICTURE CREDITS

The publishers would like to thank the following sources for their kind permission to reproduce the pictures in this book.

ALL © GETTY IMAGES
6: Sefa Karacan/Anadolu Agency; 7: Igor Russak/NurPhoto; 8: Sefa Karacan/Anadolu Agency; 10: Fabrice Coffrini/AFP; 11: Francois Nel; 14T: Mladen Antonov/AFP; 14B: Oleg Nikishin/FIFA; 15TL: Mladen Antonov/AFP; 15TR: Donat Sorokin/TASS; 15BL: Mladen Antonov/AFP; 15BR: Alexander Hassenstein/Bongarts; 16TL: Michael Regan; 16TR: Russia 2018; 16BL: Matthias Hangst; 16BR: Mladen Antonov/AFP; 17T: Michael Regan/FIFA; 17B: Matthias Hangst/Bongarts; 18: Popperfoto; 19L: Keystone/Hulton Archive; 19R: Bob Thomas; 20: Alex Livesey/FIFA; 22: Alexander Hassenstein/Bongarts; 23: Halldor Kolbeins/AFP; 24: Islam Safwat/NurPhoto; 25: Ryan Pierse; 26: Ernesto Benavides/AFP; 27: Mark Metcalfe; 29: Lars Ronbog/FrontZoneSport; 30: Amin Mohammad Jamali; 31: Mladen Antonov/AFP; 32: Dmitry Lebedev/Kommersant; 34L: Alexander Demianchuk/TASS; 34R: Sergei Savostyanov/TASS; 35L: Dean Mouhtaropoulos; 35R: Franck Fife/AFP; 36L: Dean Mouhtaropoulos; 36R: Kaz Photography; 37L: Octavio Passos; 37R: Stanley Chou; 38L: Khaled Desouki/AFP; 38R: Islam Safwat/NurPhoto; 39L: MB Media; 39R: MB Media; 40L: Adam Nurkiewicz; 40R: Luis Vera; 41L: Adam Nurkiewicz; 41R: Miguel Rojo/AFP; 42L: Carlos Rodrigues; 42R: Pedro Fiuza/NurPhoto; 43L: Ian Walton; 43R: David Ramos; 44L: Jack Guez/AFP; 44R: Claudio Villa; 45L: David Ramos; 45R: Ira L Black/Corbis; 46L: Cyrille Bah/Anadolu Agency; 46R: Fadel Senna/AFP; 47L: Fadel Senna/AFP; 47R: Fadel Senna/AFP; 48L: Power Sport Images; 48R: Amin Mohammad Jamali; 49L: Stanley Chou; 49R: Amin Mohammad Jamali; 50L: Dave Winter/Icon Sport; 50R: Nicolas Briquet/SOPA Images/LightRocket; 51L: Franck Fife/AFP; 51R: Franck Fife/AFP; 52L: Ryan Pierse; 52R: Brett Hemmings; 53L: Hector Vivas; 53R: Hector Vivas; 54L: Cris Bouroncle/AFP; 54R: Enrique Cuneo; 55L: MB Media; 55R: Cris Bouroncle/AFP; 56L: Lars Ronbog/FrontZoneSport; 56R: Lars Ronbog/FrontZoneSport; 57L: Catherine Ivill; 57R: Alex Livesey; 58L: Rodrigo Buendia/AFP; 58R: Franklin Jacome; 59L: Hector Vivas; 59R: Marcelo Endelli; 60L: Alexander Scheuber/UEFA; 60R: Haraldur Gudjonsson/AFP; 61L: MB Media; 61R: MB Media; 62L: Srdjan Stevanovic; 62R: Dan Mullan; 63L: Srdjan Stevanovic; 63R: AFP; 64L: Dan Mullan; 64R: Pius Utomi Ekpei/AFP; 65L: Catherine Ivill/AMA; 65R: Pius Utomi Ekpei/AFP; 66L: Buda Mendes; 66R: Pedro Vilela; 67L: Anthony Dibon/Icon Sport; 67R: Laurence Griffiths; 68L: Francisco Leong/AFP; 68R: Fabrice Coffrini/AFP; 69L: Attila Kisbenedek/AFP; 69R: Jean Catuffe; 70L: Mike Lawrie; 70R: Johan Ordonez/AFP; 71L: Mike Lawrie; 71R: Arnoldo Robert/LatinContent; 72L: Mladen Antonov/AFP; 72R: Srdjan Stevanovic; 73L: Andrej Isakovic/AFP; 73R: Andrej Isakovic/AFP; 74L: Alexander Hassenstein/Bongarts; 74R: Dean Mouhtaropoulos; 75L: MB Media; 75R: Matthias Hangst/Bongarts; 76L: Miguel Tovar/LatinContent; 76R: Matthew Ashton/AMA; 77L: Manuel Velasquez; 77R: Miguel Tovar/LatinContent; 78L: Nils Petter Nilsson/Ombrello; 78R: Marco Bertorello/AFP; 79L: Alessandro Sabattini; 79R: VI Images; 80L: Power Sport Images; 80R: Chung Sung-Jun; 81L: Chung Sung-Jun; 81R: Chung Sung-Jun; 82L: VI Images; 82R: Yorick Jansens/AFP; 83L: VI Images; 83R: MB Media; 84L: Stu Forster; 84R: Rodrigo Arangua/AFP; 85L: Rodrigo Arangua/AFP; 85R: Geoff Caddick/AFP; 86L: Fethi Belaid/AFP; 86R: Fethi Belaid/AFP; 87L: Visionhaus/Corbis; 87R: Visionhaus/Corbis; 88L: Dan Mullan; 88R: Mike Hewitt; 89L: Joe Klamar/AFP; 89R: MB Media; 90L: Foto Olimpik/NurPhoto; 90R: Pawel Andrachiewicz/PressFocus/MB Media; 91L: Andrew Surma/NurPhoto; 91R: Lukasz Laskowski/PressFocus; 92L: Seyllou/AFP; 92R: Seyllou/AFP; 93L: Visionhaus/Corbis; 93R: Catherine Ivill/AMA; 94L: Gabriel Aponte/LatinContent; 94R: Guillermo Legaria/LatinContent; 95L: William Volcov/LatinContent; 95R: Jose Breton/NurPhoto; 96L: Hiroki Watanabe; 96R: The Asahi Shimbun; 97L: MB Media; 97R: Amin M Jamali; 98: Eitan Abramovich/AFP; 100: Quinn Rooney; 101: VI Images; 102: Ramsey Cardy/Sportsfile; 103: Chris Brunskill Ltd; 104: Etsuo Hara; 105: Mike Hewitt; 106: Foto Olimpik/NurPhoto; 107: Epsilon; 108: Mladen Antonov/AFP; 109: Mike Lawrie; 110: Pressefoto Ulmer/ullstein bild; 111: Etsuo Hara; 112: Jean Catuffe; 113: Franck Fife/AFP; 114: Ahmed Awaad/NurPhoto; 115: Sandro Pereyra/LatinContent; 116: Alex Livesey; 118: Popperfoto; 119T: Martin Rose; 119B: Mike Powell; 120L: Claudio Villa; 120R: Allsport; 121: Bob Thomas; 122: Popperfoto; 123: Koji Aoki/AFLO

Page 13: Courtesy of adidas

Every effort has been made to acknowledge correctly and contact the source and/or copyright holder of each picture and Carlton Books Limited apologizes for any unintentional errors or omissions that will be corrected in future editions of this book.